Memoirs of a Hustler

Hustler

Stories from the Road

CJ Wiley

Copyright © 2025

All Rights Reserved

Dedication

This book is dedicated to my mother, June, who made sure I had the tools to reach my full potential; my sister, Tatha, who influenced me to be a Renaissance Man; my many mentors, who taught me some of life's challenging lessons; and finally, the game of pool, which made my dreams possible, by being my greatest teacher.

Contents

Dedication 3

About the Author 6

Preface 7

Foreword Uncovering the Perfection of the Game 1

CHAPTER 1 4

    The Early Years 4

    The Teenage Years 11

    First Road Trip – Columbia, Missouri 18

    High School Daze 21

    Turning the Tables in Burlington, Iowa 27

    On the Road with Craig Bickford (1982) 31

    Hustling the Popo in Waukegan, Illinois (1982) 36

    Learning How to Win the Big Cash Endurance Matches 41

    Underworld Elements of Gambling (1983) 48

    How Steve Mizerak Crushed My Basketball Career (1983) 52

CHAPTER 2 56

    Early Road Lessons from the Master's (1983) 56

    Hustled by Jacksonville Harley (1983) 66

    How to Outsmart the Bandits (1984) 69

    The North Carolina Hustle (1984) 75

    My Best Undercover Names (1984) 78

    Now or Never Moment (1984) 80

    Turning Lemons into Lemonade in Atlanta (1984) 85

    On the Road with a Jewel named Zia (1984) 88

    Zen Master & Pool Hustler, Dalton Leong (1983/84) 94

    The Corporations (1984) 102

    The Rack, Detroit, Michigan (1984) 106

CHAPTER 3 118

    Battling the Columbians for Big Money in Miami, Florida ... 118

    Adventures at the Doll House in Fort Lauderdale, Florida 121

    Hustling Kentucky with a Call Girl (1986) 124

    Battling Matlock with "Boom Boom," Billy Johnson 126

    Death Left and the Synchronistic Path (1986) 129

    Bizarre Killer Pilot Flies Plane with Flat Tires (1986) 133

    World Series of Tavern Pool in Las Vegas, Nevada (1986) 139

    The Real Color of Money (1987) 145

    Stabbed (1988) 150

About the Author

CJ Wiley is a celebrated pool player renowned for his exceptional skill and strategic prowess. With numerous tournament victories under his belt, CJ has cemented his reputation as one of the top players in the world of billiards. His career highlights include winning the prestigious 1996 ESPN World Open Championship, conquering The Million Dollar Pool Challenge, and earning the title of Pro Player of the Year during his competitive years. Known for his engaging and charismatic personality, CJ has captivated audiences both on and off the table. In his memoir, he takes readers on a thrilling journey through the raw and riveting world of professional pool hustling, sharing captivating stories from a life dedicated to mastering the art of the game.

Preface

I intend to share my knowledge about competition, myself, and the game in this book. In doing so, I may address issues that go against what's commonly taught or thought. From my personal experience, there is an evolutionary process to understanding; things that make sense now may not have had the same meaning years, weeks, or even days ago. One of the most extraordinary things about pocket billiards is how many levels there are to master and how much the game teaches us as a microcosm of life.

For me, the game may be pool; for you, it may be another unique quality you possess or want to excel at—business, sports, education, parenting, relationships, or anything else that can be an analogy to pocket billiards. The Game became my teacher, and I couldn't have picked a better one. In my later years, I learned that we didn't choose some of our most excellent teachers in life; they were possibly selected for us. Looking back, it almost seems like an advanced group of angelic architects laid out my path so I'd meet the right mentor in the ideal place and time.

CJ Wiley.

Foreword
Uncovering the Perfection of the Game

An elderly gentleman appeared in my life over 30 years ago for a brief parenthesis in my reality and gifted me a present that I now realize was perfectly timed. Was it the irony of fate?

I was standing behind the bar I owned in Dallas, Texas, which was unusual since I was not a bartender (especially during business hours). An elderly man unassumingly entered the door and quietly sat at the bar before us.

"Would you like a drink? I'm a champion bartender," I said, trying to keep a straight face. The bartender said playfully, "As long as you just want a bottled beer or Pepsi."

Seeing we were enjoying a private joke, the gentleman beamed and replied, "I'll just have a bottle of water. Thanks." The bartender reached into the cooler for water as the man directed his gaze back to me. "I think you might be a better pool player than a bartender. Would you agree?"

"I think you have a good point there, partner. If I had to rely on my bar-tending skills, I'd be sleeping in the streets," I said, smiling uneasily. The man's eyes were clear and very bright, it almost seemed like he was looking at a video of my thoughts inside my mind.

"You are the professional pool player who owns this place. I've seen you play before," he said. I nodded, still adjusting to the intensity of the man's crystal blue eyes. His voice remained soft, almost soothing.

"What do you expect to achieve from your pool game?" he asked, motioning to the Brunswick table just left of the front door, where he had entered only minutes before.

"I guess I would like to compete with the world's best players and maybe even beat a couple of them," I again smiled, but inside, my mind was busy running through thousands of memories. It seemed like I had known this man before, but from where?

No memories seemed to match; I had a strange déjà vu sensation, like, "This has happened before."

The man laid his open napkin on the bar before us and looked back at me. "You know that game is perfect, don't you?" he said, looking back at the napkin on the bar and then quickly back at me.

"Perfect?" I ask, "What do you mean? If you're asking if I play the game perfectly, the answer is no, but I have these moments-" my eyes lose focus as I instinctively reminisce about the feeling of being in the *The Zone*.

He shook his head and chuckled slightly, "You're human, young man. Perfection is not in your nature. However, it is in the game. The Game is perfect at the highest level." The man lifted the napkin on the bar, appeared to look under it for something, and quickly placed it back. "You have to uncover that perfection like this napkin uncovers the treasures beneath it!"

He looked back into my now-refocused eyes. "Do you understand? He lifted the napkin again as if treasure were buried underneath, and then put it back down. "Perfection is in the Game, and you must be the one to uncover it. Perfection will play through you; the Game can only express its perfection, like an instrument, through people that play."

Other things were said, but the memories trail off like a dream. In my memory, the man just disappeared, but I'm sure he got up and walked out of the poolroom that day like a regular person, or did he?

It took me several years to understand what that intriguing man with those crystal blue eyes meant by "the perfection of the Game playing through me." However, the seed began to grow, and over time, it started making more and more sense, leading to the most satisfying discovery of my career.

CHAPTER 1

THE EARLY YEARS

My first memory of pocket billiards is watching Minnesota Fats and Willie Mosconi play on ABC's Wide World of Sports with Howard Cosell as the commentator. I used to watch Willie Mosconi appear angry while Minnesota Fats told his stories; he was a showboat and a fascinating storyteller. I dreamed of meeting the fat man; he was larger than life to me. I didn't realize it, but there would be a day when not only would I meet Minnesota Fats, but he would give me one of my greatest compliments. I only dreamed of being a world-champion pool player when I used to watch Fats, but to warm up for a major tournament with Fats watching me would have been far-fetched, even for a dream.

I grew up in Green City, Missouri. It had a population of 629 and was so small that it didn't have a single stoplight. We lived on the edge of town in a farming community, and we had about four acres. Approximately an acre was used as a lumberyard that my father owned.

My parents, with a sizeable lawn and house, farmed the other three acres. The garden consisted of corn, radishes, strawberries, lettuce, green beans, carrots, and a few blackberry bushes. My mother ended up having the job of picking vegetables, and we grew enough food not only to feed us but also to sell to people in the community to make a little extra money.

We lived in a big two-story house with three bedrooms and a basement. I think my parents paid $12,000 for the property and home. My father had access to carpenters and supplies through his lumberyard, so he improved the property and added a large deck that wrapped halfway around the side of the house. Since my sister was fourteen years older than I was, she had left for college by the time I was four, so I grew up primarily as an only child.

Green City had a Town Square made up of various businesses. My mother worked at City Hall, which stood in the middle of the town square, where she kept the city's books. She was a kind and loving mother but had little time to be idle between her work, mowing the lawn, and tending to the spacious garden.

My father, on the other hand, was an alcoholic. The tension in our home stemmed from a deep hatred my mother had for my father, which she tried to shield me from. A few years before I was born, my father drove to the local truck stop to drink with some buddies while my mom was visiting relatives. After a whole night of drinking, one of my father's friends brought him home and threw him on the couch, passed out.

After waking the following day, my father got a ride back to the truck stop to retrieve his vehicle, taking my three-year-old baby sister, Wendy, along reluctantly. Maybe it was because he had a hangover, or maybe it was just a random accident; Wendy was hit by a truck while running across the parking lot and killed instantly.

I believe this accident had a major psychological effect on my father, and he and I were never very close since he was a truck driver, drinker, and gone most of the time. When he was home, he had me drill holes in metal plates that connected farm equipment, like hay feeders, troughs, and sawhorses. After paying me a little for the work, he would make me play poker and either take all my money or I'd take his. He didn't stop until all the money was won.

Looking back on my early childhood, I can see where the urge to make a living gambling came from. Since my parents were often gone, I learned how to deal with loneliness and boredom. My escape was playing any game involving a ball and the thrill of controlling it like it was an extension of myself.

As I got older and began first grade, a group of my friends and I discussed going to the town square and playing pool at Cleeton's Poolhall. Surrounding the outside of the square were a little cafe, an auto parts store, a grocery store, a bank, a city hall, and an insurance company. I hadn't been to the pool room yet, so it was exciting to think about going there. I often walked to school through the snow in the winter months, which was about a quarter mile, and a little further was Cleeton's.

On Saturday mornings, I'd arrive at 7:00 when Orin, the owner, was opening. Orrin was an older man and the father of

Grumpy Cleeton, a friend of my mother and father. So, when I first started going to the poolroom, my mother talked to him, and he promised to keep an eye on me and ensure I didn't get into trouble.

When I first entered Cleeton's, the smell was memorable; it was a mixture of smoke and chewing tobacco and hit me like a brick in the face as I entered through the door. The dimly lit room had dingy floors, a theater-style ceiling, and three 9-foot Brunswick Centennial tables covered in different-colored cloth. The first was red, the next was green, and the last was blue. I think they might have switched that a time or two, but those were the colors that I remember.

In the back of the room was an old wood-burning stove like the ones you see in an old country home, with a small room just adjacent to the stove where the men would play gin-rummy during the day. Scanning the room, I saw spittoons, just metal buckets scattered around, for men to spit their tobacco into. Many people smoked, so the smell of a poolroom wasn't the greatest smell to most people, but I liked it strangely. To this day, I associate smoking with pool, so secondhand smoke has never bothered me. I have fond memories of it.

During winter, I would help Mr. Orrin bring in wood; the poolroom would be freezing, so the balls would be like little spheres of ice. I remember how cold they were to my small hands, as I would grab them from the bottom chute and put them on the table. The balls seemed to come to life as the room began to warm up. Cold pool balls don't react well; they are dead to the strike. It wasn't much fun playing until the room reached a specific temperature.

In those days, one game would cost you a dime, and you only paid if you lost. For me, this was a big incentive to get better and not lose, and looking back, it introduced me to my first form of gambling. I would play all day and not spend a single cent on pool. Sometimes, on Saturdays, I would go there early in the morning. I'd play all day and never lose a game, so it didn't cost me anything except to buy a toaster sandwich and peanuts to pour in my bottle of Pepsi.

This didn't go over so well with the older kids. They didn't like getting beaten by an eight-year-old, so they would hide my bicycle while I was playing. At the end of the day, when I went outside, I'd have to look for it. I'd first head across the street to the bank. That's where they usually put it, or it would be a bit farther down the street in one of the ditches.

I hated the feeling; it was a shameful experience. I knew it was one of the older, spiteful kids. Since the poolroom was on a Town Square, there were several places where my bicycle would end up, but I always found it. The situation was a bummer, and I had no brothers or sisters to help me navigate these new foreign experiences or protect me from the incessant bullying I would receive throughout my early school years.

We decided to go to the poolroom one day after our classes. One of the kids, Rod Dixon, had played pool before, and he challenged me to a game. He and I were two of the top athletes in our class for basketball and baseball, so we both had excellent hand-eye coordination. I will never forget how nervous I was around the older kids and several old men who played gin daily in the back room.

My friends and I were too short to reach the pool table, so we stood on wooden Pepsi crates. They were 16-oz bottles, so the crates were probably a foot high. With the extra height, we could reach the table. I'm so glad Orrin had me stand on the crates because I never had to shoot with the cue stick directly on my chin.

Because of this early experience, I now shoot a few inches higher, which has made it easier for my back and neck and certainly never hurt my shot-making ability. We played three games, and I surprisingly won all three. Looking back, I had such a knack for the game, like I may have been predestined to play — I have grown to believe fate was involved for so many unusual dots to connect!

Later, my mother and father bought me a small pool table with balls about the size of ping-pong balls for our house. I could play alone and spend hours in my sister's room, where the pool table was set up, imagining I was four different characters. I was Carson, CJ, Wiley, and, lastly, a Mexican man from Texas with a giant sombrero and a thick mustache. He looked like Juan Valdez from the coffee commercial on TV in the 1980s.

I thought it was more than a coincidence that I imagined I was playing with this Mexican guy from Texas. I eventually ended up moving to Texas and meeting many people who looked a lot like him. We didn't have many ethnicities in Green City, and I was raised to see everyone as the same racially.

The first time our basketball team played another team with a black guy on it, the gymnasium was packed; they were hanging off the rafters to see this player. The funny part was he ended up being short, maybe five foot eight, but could still dunk a basketball, which he did warming up, and it sounded like he got a standing ovation; you'd have thought Michael Jordan had made a double reverse dunk to win the title. Looking back, that was comical.

By the time I was nine years old and could run a rack of Eight-Ball on a nine-foot table – I was one of the better players in my small town of Green City and a few surrounding towns. I could run the table but couldn't draw my cue ball (using low English). I remember asking a man in the poolroom who eventually became my high school principal, also a pretty good shot, to teach me how to use low English to draw the ball.

I'd watch him draw his ball by putting low English on the cue and making it spin back down the table. I thought that was so cool. I courageously asked him if he would show me how to do it one day. He refused and told me that it would hurt my game, which, looking back, was not exactly an honest statement. Back then, pool players guarded secrets like a precious stone.

As the years went by, I started playing better and better, and at the age of twelve, I broke and ran all fifteen balls in order from one through the fifteen on a nine-foot pool table. That's still, to this day, a difficult thing to do. During the winter, pool was my primary focus; however, I played tennis competitively in the summer and worked weekends to make extra money.

I started a small snowcone business at the age of 10, which was quite lucrative, especially for a young child. Every weekend, I would pack four coolers with crushed ice and go to the local farmer's market, farm sales, or flea markets. My mother clerked the farm sales while I set up a stand and sold snow cones for $.50 each. We would make about $60 per cooler and bring home, on average, about $200 per day that we worked.

By the time I turned sixteen, I had saved over $20,000, enough to buy a car, which was just an orange Pinto, but I loved the freedom it gave me. I later purchased a Ford Tempo Diesel that got 57 mpg; I could fill it up for twelve dollars and go over six hundred miles. I put over a hundred and fifty thousand miles on it and ultimately left it at a gas station in Southern Illinois when the timing belt broke; that car had more than paid for itself many times.

THE TEENAGE YEARS

One of my few bonding experiences with my father was when I was eleven. My dad took me to play tennis. I had seen Bjorn Borg, Jimmy Connors, and other players on TV, but I had never played the game myself. We went to Unionville, Missouri, about 35 miles from Green City. I remember two courts in a small park with backstops and a chain-link fence around them.

We got on one of the courts and started to play. My dad had played tennis before because his family in Iowa had a dirt court, and they used to have the neighborhood kids come over. He played and showed me the basics of how to hold the racquet and make the swing.

I didn't do so well, but I liked it. I just hadn't developed the stroke yet, so I went back home and started practicing and swinging the tennis racket with a cover on it repeatedly. I always tried to emulate some of the players I'd seen on TV. I purchased Tennis Magazine that showed me the basics, so the second time my dad and I played, I did better.

The third time we played, I started playing better than he did, so I was hooked! Tennis was a great way to develop my right arm, wrist, and fingers. There was a period when my right forearm looked noticeably bigger than my left and was substantially stronger from hitting thousands of balls. Tennis enhanced me physically, which showed up in other sports like basketball and baseball, and mentally as well when I read the book Inner Tennis by Tim Gallaway.

My Dad ended up making me a dirt tennis court in the backyard. We had four acres, so behind his lumberyard, he bulldozed the land where it was pretty level and put up two backstops to catch the balls. I didn't have anybody to play with, so I purchased a Prince Ball machine, which I learned to use from Terry Taylor, a tennis coach who had taught lessons at the local school gymnasium. He set up a net on the basketball court and offered a clinic for anyone interested in learning.

He must have seen some potential in me because I got his number and went and saw him again. He started working with me and invited me to be his assistant during the summer, teaching tennis lessons across Northern Missouri. We traveled in a black 49' Plymouth with a huge trunk. We could fit two Prince Ball machines and all the balls and rackets in that trunk.

We were on the road — that's the first time I went on the road playing tennis; the pool would come a couple of years later. One of the highlights of our travels was spending a lot of time in Bowling Green, Missouri. It was centrally located, and it was easy for people to travel twenty or thirty miles from different parts of the state to take his clinics, so we stayed there more than in other towns.

There, I met a state patrolman named Norm, a tennis player. I remember he was there one day, and I was hitting serves; he got his speed gun out to measure my serve. I hit the serve at ninety-one mph, which surprised a lot of the adults because Terry Taylor, I think, was only hitting about ninety-seven, which is pretty darn fast!

I had an exceptional right arm, and that's why I pitched so effectively in baseball. In the finals of a little league tournament, I threw a no-hitter—nobody hit the ball at all, and there were only two foul balls in the whole game! The other team didn't touch the ball the entire game with a bat, and I hit two home runs—I hit 17 home runs the last year I played Little League Baseball.

Pitching was my forte, and several people were scouting me, especially Don Albertson, who urged me to become a professional baseball pitcher, but I preferred individual sports. My pursuit of pool mastery was on hold during the summer months. I remember going to the poolroom during tennis season. It was hot, and there was no air conditioning in Cleeton's poolroom, so it wasn't appealing. That was my schedule for several years; I went with Terry Taylor two years in a row to teach tennis, and my game kept improving.

Kirksville, Missouri, was about twenty miles from Green City. My mother would take me to the tennis courts there, and I would just hit balls by myself, hitting serves back and forth with three rock-hard orange tennis balls. I had worn the fuzz off by playing with them so much, hitting against any wall I could find. Then I'd go up to the school and hit balls against a wall that they had in the back of the school, which had fine gravel so that when the ball hit the ground, it wasn't predictable where it would bounce.

This practice helped to sharpen my speed and reflexes. I always had a knack for any game that required a ball. However, I was never very good at bowling. Around this time, I met John Emerick on the tennis court while hitting three rock-hard orange tennis balls.

John had just finished with the Kirksville tennis team and was getting ready to ride his bike to work. He was walking by and stopped to watch me for a bit. He seemed impressed that this young kid would hit serves repeatedly and have nobody to play with, so he asked me if I would like to play. I beamed when he asked because I'd been waiting to play with someone since I mostly played alone. He put down his things and hit balls with me for about fifteen minutes since he had to leave for work at the Menn's Tea House, a little Chinese restaurant off the square in downtown Kirksville.

We exchanged phone numbers, and I got to know him well. We eventually became best friends even though he lived 20 miles away from me. My mother would take me over on Friday nights, and I would spend the weekend with John and play tennis with him or shoot pool at a local bowling alley. We also found some other people to play with, and then my mother would come, get me on Sunday night, and take me back to Green City.

When I wasn't playing tennis, my friends and I would play pool at Leisure World or another bowling alley named Lucky Lanes. For money games, I'd go to the Pro Bass Shop. It was a small hunting supply store and archery range, and I think the guy who owned it was related to those who opened the Bass Pro Shop chain. This little place sold all the hunting and fishing gear in the front, but as you got to the rear of the store, three nine-foot tables stood in a small pool room; they also had a Three Cushion Billiard table, and the archery range was through another door in the remaining side of the building.

I met a few gamblers in Kirksville when I played at Leisure World who would use a lot of little one-liners that kept you laughing. Something I always liked about poolrooms was the larger-than-life characters. To me, pool players are just naturally funny. Max, a guy I played with at the Pro Bass Shop, and I used to go to the 7-Eleven right around the corner late at night and gamble playing pinball.

He was a good pinball player and used to spot me some points so that I would gamble with him. We would gamble against some locals, win as much as $100 a night, and split the winnings. When you were fifteen, that was a lot of money in those days, and we would play pinball and gamble all night. This is where I began to get seasoned in the art of wagering.

Then, one night at Leisure World, some friends came in and told me that a big-time pool player from Columbia, Missouri, named Tom Draper, was in town and looking to gamble. Columbia was about 90 miles south of Kirksville, a much bigger city with a large University. My friends figured he was pretty good, so they came and got me to play him. All my friends had stopped playing with me for money a year before, so I was excited that someone wanted to gamble.

We introduced ourselves, and he said he wanted to play 9-ball. I told him I didn't know how to play 9-ball and that I played 15-ball. Rotation, where you hit balls in their numeric order: one, two, three, etc., and keep score of points. Nevertheless, I mainly played 8-ball then, so he agreed to that game, and we flipped for the break. I broke and ran three racks in a row.

This got old Tom steaming, and he started pressing me to play 9-ball with him since I had just beat him out of $100. I was reluctant to play since I did not know the game and refused, but he kept pressing me. I knew he didn't have a chance, but it was always strategic and even fun playing hard to get. I agreed to play 9-ball but needed him to explain to me how to play. He accused me of hustling him even though I didn't know the rules, but he continued looking for some advantage he could use to get his money back.

I still had the break from the previous game, so I cracked them and ran all the balls on the table in order from one through nine. His face turned beet red, and his voice quivered as he accused me of hustling him again, but after a while, he calmed down. I pointed out that I didn't want to play 9-ball, but he urged me to play. This seemed to satisfy his feelings about my alleged deception. After all, you can't hustle an honest man. I was just fifteen, so naturally, he thought he had a great game, but as the old timers used to say, hunting is no fun when the rabbit has the gun!

As Tom was packing up his cue, I was curious. There was something about this guy; he seemed like someone I could make some money with. "Hey Tom, I'm curious about the competition up in Columbia. I know there's some good players down there, and I was thinking about taking a road trip." Tom replied, "That's a great idea. Come on down, and I'll take you around and introduce you to the people you need to know."

He told me about the Columbia Billiard Center and how many gamblers hung out there, like BJ the mailman, Craig, Donnie, Keith, Fuzzy, and One-Eyed Red. We exchanged numbers, and Tom was on his way. I just needed to secure a car to get me there and figure out how to explain it to my mom since I didn't have a driver's license.

When I was fifteen, my game was already seasoned; I had won my first regional tournament in a little bar about twenty-five miles away when I was twelve. My dad took me to compete in that tournament, and I still remember playing in the finals. I played another young kid; he might have been three or four years older than me.

We played on a bar table, which is seven feet long. I was used to playing on a nine-foot table. Playing on the smaller version was a piece of cake. I won that tournament and got my first pool trophy at twelve. That's when I started making headway with my pool game and ran my first rack of rotation, the one through the fifteen in numeric order. It is still challenging to do it; the most I've run is three in a row; this was in Baltimore, and on the fourth rack, I ran down to four balls on the table and hooked myself by a hair. Growing up with 8-ball and 15-ball Rotation, my game had the best of both worlds. The Filipino players love Rotation, and the rules are much more challenging than how 9-ball is played today with the one-foul rule.

First Road Trip – Columbia, Missouri

I approached my friend from tennis, John Emerick, after we played the following week after meeting Tom. "Listen, I need to borrow your car to drive to Columbia. Is that something we can arrange?"

"Why do you want to go to Columbia, and you do realize you don't have a license, right?"

"Man, I've been driving since I was twelve. I met this guy from Columbia at Leisure World the other night and beat him out of some cash. He told me, steering me, that there were some excellent scores there at the Columbia Billiard Center.

"Do you think you can win against them? It's a big city; there's got to be some top-notch players!"

I assured him, "Yeah, no problem, especially if they play like Tom; he said some suckers play under his speed."

"Okay, I'll loan you my car, but if you wreck it, you pay for it."

I agreed since I had saved over $12,000 from my snow cone business, and he knew I would never break my word to him. To this very day, I haven't, and we have had many financial dealings together throughout the years. Eight years later, we even bought a house together in Carrolton, Texas.

"Okay, man, that's fair enough. If I wreck it, I'll pay," I promised. John had a little yellow Mazda, and I drove it ninety miles to Columbia, to the Columbia Billiards Center, a little place on 9th Street. There, I had my first gambling game with Keith, a tall, dark-headed guy, about twenty-six, carrying himself like a hotshot.

I discovered later that Keith was one of the best players in the area. I started strong, my heart racing with excitement; there was something about playing pool for money that stimulated every sense. I played strong, beating him out of $120, playing 9-Ball for $20 a game.

Keith began to unscrew his cue and pack up, "I need some weight to play you; you're better than me."

"Weight, what is weight?" I asked with genuine curiosity.

"You know what weight is. Don't be hustling me." He'd been around, but I honestly didn't know what this term meant, which, I came to find out, means handicap or "a spot" in pool lingo.

"How much weight do you need?" I asked, knowing he was probably going to get the best of the game. However, I was ahead of him, so I had everything to win, playing with his money.

Keith proposed, "If you give me the seven, eight, nine, I win on those three balls; you just win on the nine. I can make it on the break and make combinations on any of the three balls."

I considered it briefly and agreed, "That sounds fair." So, I gave him the seven, eight, and nine. Initially, I was ahead, but then he started making them on the break and lucky combinations.

The weight started to take its toll. I was wearing down (trying to carry the weight), so we ended up even, and I quit.

"I can't give you this much weight anymore," I said.

This wasn't exactly true because I later gave him the six-ball on a seven-foot table and ran five racks in a row on him. He got a shot, and then I ran five more racks in a row on him, and he quit, saying, "I will never play you again!" That's how the next level of my gambling career took place, and it all started at Columbia Billiards.

I would go there quite a bit, staying with some of the generous locals who gave me accommodation and hanging out with those older guys who mature me up to many things. I also started dating a girl named Kelli Reynolds, who looked like a Playboy centerfold with the body to match. She was a hustler herself. We went on some successful road trips and ended up working for an intelligence agency with a top-secret security clearance, but that's another story. I'd never experienced this stuff in the small town of Green City; I was learning what I'd later call a PHD, a pool hall degree, which is about street wisdom, not book smarts.

HIGH SCHOOL DAZE

I had been out in the gambling world, on the road, and I started questioning how much of the information they were teaching us in school would apply to real life. I was bored of memorizing stuff for tests and started to act up, which put me in the principal's office. The principal was named Gary, and he was the same man who told me it would hurt my pool game if I learned how to use low English. I remember him asking me what I would do with my life when I was sent to him for my less-than-good behavior.

"You know you're messing up in school, and you'll need to go to college to make something of yourself," He gave me the college sales pitch for about ten minutes; I had no intention of going, so I drowned his voice out thinking to myself I'd rather be anywhere but here listening to this loser!

"I'm going to be a professional pool player," I said when I heard a break in his rhetoric.

He scoffed. "Yeah, right, what if you get your eye put out?" I replied in a rebellious tone,

"My eye put out? What if you get your eye put out?" It's amazing the lengths people will go to conform to the system and influence kids to do the same. Meanwhile, most of our history influencers didn't attend college or even go all the way through high school.

I stayed in a little room beside his office the rest of the period, daydreaming about the pool and this cute girl I'd met in Columbia who had my attention; Kelli liked her too, which was even more enticing. One thing I knew was that I didn't fit in very well in school, and nobody seemed to encourage me to do anything other than go back to school, which didn't make any sense. I am proud that I was rebellious; he didn't stop me from pursuing my aspirations to become a champion pool player.

A couple of weeks later, I saw a chance to play in the National High School championships, but to do so, I had to qualify for a regional tournament held at Raytown Recreation. Raytown is a small suburb of Kansas City. Don Brink was the owner, and he was a three-cushion billiard champion, a really good player. I planned to go to Raytown and drive there, about a hundred and fifty miles from where I was in Green City.

I had reached the finals of the Missouri State Championships when I was 17 the previous year and was getting more of a reputation on the road; hustling pool and gambling and being around many older, wiser men was rubbing off. High school was getting boring. Looking back, there were just a lot of things we had to memorize that never came up in life, but what I learned on the road did come up and would benefit me in ways I would never have dreamed of in multi-million-dollar businesses.

Kansas City was about a three-hour drive from Green City, which wasn't far, considering I'd been driving to Omaha, Nebraska, to Big Johns since I was old enough to drive. I packed up some tuna salad my mom had made and some turkey, tomatoes, onions, bread, and Ranch dressing so I didn't have to stop for food. I loaded up the car, put in some Led Zepplin, and was on the road again; the thoughts of what might happen were overwhelming. I was confident against any high school kid, but out of all the players in Missouri, I was sure there would be some stiff competition.

I love driving, and many of my most extensive improvements in the pool came to me during a long drive; I'd often exercise my imagination by pretending to shoot one star into the moon or another star using the steering wheel as the cue ball. One time, as a challenge, I drove from Green City to Omaha without touching the steering wheel with my hands, which required playing great position because it's hard to make sharp turns; I could do it using my knees and sometimes even my feet.

This trip, I'd keep my hands on the wheel; I wanted to arrive in one piece. Raytown Recreation was an old-time poolroom with about twelve nine-foot billiard tables and one ten-footer right up in front. The poolroom was underground; I found the address, parked about a block away, got my cue, walked down the street to the entrance, opened the door, and looked down the stairs.

I could feel the anticipation as I walked down the stairs and into the poolroom. The first thing I saw was the ten-foot table; the room was packed, with many young players scattered all over it. I made my way to the tournament desk to sign up. I could feel a buzz going around the room. I'd played there before. Their best player was Steve Hassell. He was better than me, but I still broke even with him when we gambled.

It was cool to be respected for my talent and even feared. I had felt that in tennis and pitching baseball, but it was more because I threw so hard and hit tennis balls fast and sometimes directly at my opponent; with pool, mental intimidation is the significant intimidation factor; we call it the "feint factor" because if someone can't handle pressure, they will feint!

I reached the desk and waited for the lady to finish something she was writing.

"My name is CJ Wiley. Is this where I need to check in?"

The lady looked at me and smiled, "You made it. I've heard a lot about you."

"Really, well, if any of it was bad, it's not true!" she beamed. I have some great news for you. Because of your reputation and how you did in the Men's State Tournament in Columbia, we have decided to give you the qualifying spot, and everyone will play today for an additional spot in Nationals."

"You're kidding, so I don't have to put my cue together?"

"I'm sure many people would like to see you play; maybe you can show off a little on the ten-foot table. I'm sure several players would love to play a few games."

So that's what I did: I practiced with several locals. I like the ten-foot table; it requires more of a stroke, and when I return to nine-footers, it gives me an advantage. My game is always better when my stroke feels more powerful. I also like to practice with a heavy or bigger cue ball. My favorite practice device involves using a thick rubber band to strengthen my stroke.

I still wonder why the other kids didn't want to play against me; after all, it's not like I could hit them with a ball or anything, but the rumors were circulating about me, and I'm not sure what they were saying. Still, whatever it was, it got me past the Missouri State qualifier, now on to Rockford, Illinois, which was about a five-hour drive from home, but this time, I would call and make sure, who knows, maybe they would give me a pass in the regional tournament as well, the thought of that made me laugh out loud.

I found the poolroom number in Rockford, and sure enough, they told me I didn't have to come; they would give me a spot and play the qualifier for another one. This was amazing; I'd won State and Regionals without hitting a single ball, but now I was in the main national high-school tournament, so there was no chance I'd get any preferential treatment there. However, the thought of winning was appealing, although I still expected to have my hands full.

The National High School Championships were held in a big hotel ballroom in Arlington Heights at the same time as the United States Pro Championships. Since I was used to playing with adults and not high school kids, I decided to play in a professional mini-tournament. I ultimately lost against Earl Strickland for a chance to play in the finals. Earl was starting to make a name for himself and came in second. Mike Massie won the professional tournament and put on a trick shot exhibition. It was an incredible show to watch. He mixed pool shots with magic, "finger pool," and card tricks. He was quite an entertainer and a genuinely good-hearted man.

When the High School Championship started, it was a race to five games. I plowed through the competition, getting used to playing professional and semi-pro adults. When I reached the finals, I had only lost one game the whole day. My opponent and I went back and forth. The finals were two out of three sets, but I think the pressure of playing in the finals got to him, and I was now the National High School Champion.

I didn't receive many accolades when I returned to my little town of Green City, although the principal gave me a big, fake smile and told me, "Way to represent!" I knew he didn't mean it as a compliment; pool was still looked down on as a seedy underground sport, but I have to see at those Nationals what it was like to play in front of a large crowd and be under that kind of pressure. I loved the feeling, especially the pressure, not on me as much as the pressure I could put on other players. From my experience, this was what high-level competition was all about.

Turning the Tables in Burlington, Iowa

I had been playing on the road, mainly in Missouri and some cities in Illinois, Kansas, and Iowa, so rumors about me were circulating in the gambling world. Since it was 1981, there was no Internet, so they don't know what I look like. John Emerick and I concocted a plan to take a road trip to Burlington, Iowa, and switch identities. He became CJ Wiley, and I became John

Emerick to trick some suckers into playing us for money. I pulled some strings to get us information about the Sportsman Club, a place known for gambling, and prearranged the identity switch ahead of time.

This worked out well, except for one thing. The only way they would play us was 9-ball, with us giving them the eight-ball handicap. In other words, they would win if they made the eight or nine ball. Additionally, they would not play CJ (John) but me, the actual CJ. I agreed to their terms and gave the guy the eight ball.

Unknown to me then, the Sportsman Club had its share of professionals and road players doing the hustling moves and tricks weekly. So, whenever strangers came through, it was known not to believe them at face value. Unfortunately, for me, my opponent played much better than I expected. We played $50 per game, and he turned the tables on me and beat me out of all my money, about $400, which was a substantial amount, but I still had my Meucci cue stick, which had a lot of value and my only option to get more money to gamble.

There was no doubt that I was off my game that day. When some road players get down, they usually try to "air barrel" or play one last set while broke and not tell their opponent, but I had never done that and instead said, "Hey guys, I'm busted, but I would like to put up my cue and keep playing." Terry, one of the bar owners, loved that cue as soon as he saw it. It was a beautiful, five-point custom cue made by Bob Meucci with golden diamonds inlaid along the base and perfectly weighted for my game. I bought that cue with the money I had made from selling snow cones, and it was one of my most prized possessions.

Another patron, Mitch, who I later became friends with, said, "Terry, don't buy that damn cue!" However, Terry had to have it and bought it on the spot. He gave me $200, and I walked over to the wall and grabbed a house cue. The best stick I could find was slightly bent and had a well-worn tip almost down to the wood it was glued to.

I leaned over the table, took a deep breath, and broke the balls. From there, I won almost every game, got all my money back, and won another couple hundred; I had escaped the trap! Walking over to Terry, the bar owner, I repurchased my prized cue, much to his dismay. Sometimes, as a road player, you get robbed in a game, but the trick is to use our strategic abilities and put the "re-rob" on them; I had a lot of tricks up my sleeve, especially for a teenage kid.

When I finally got home from my road trip, things were different; my perception had gained a lot of knowledge and experiences quickly. The thought of going back to school wasn't appealing at all. My trip started at Christmas break, and I decided that going back was impossible. There was nothing left to learn there for me.

My mother thought college was a good option. My sister went all the way through to get her PhD in theology. She studied 40+ hours a week and made straight as in every class; she was given a medal for her academic achievements and wrote several books. I never felt as intelligent as my sister. She was so dedicated and extremely book-smart and I told my mom when we were discussing why I wasn't going back to high school after my road trip.

Her answer surprised me and even shocked me because she rarely complimented me. She wanted me to have self-confidence and not rely on other people's praise or compliments for my self-esteem.

"You're smarter than she is," she said bluntly.

I didn't ask why or how she made that determination; the compliment was taken in stride, but I always remember her saying it and knew she was being honest—she was like that—always direct and to the point. Looking back, she never sugarcoated anything, and I appreciated that about her. My education was much better when I explained that school wasn't an option. I traveled and learned from my gambling and hustling experiences. I also had a lot of business knowledge from running my snow cone stand for eight years.

I packed up my car and headed to Columbia, Missouri, to meet Craig Bickford. When I returned to the house, my mother sat at the kitchen table in deep thought. I knew she was concerned about my safety, especially carrying a lot of cash and hustling many people. Still, she trusted and encouraged me to follow my instincts and intuition.

I told her my goodbyes, and she stood up and took a few steps toward me. She looked concerned and said, "Just remember one thing, CJ. There will always be someone better coming along, so be careful." She warned sincerely.

"Yes, Mom, but I may be that someone!"

Her concerned face broke into a smile. Her eyes twinkled, and she said, "Yes, I know."

We hugged. She gave me one last look as I turned to walk out that door for the last time. I knew there would be nowhere to come back to. Now that I was leaving, my mother would sell the house and divorce my father. She only stayed with him for so long because she wanted to see me grow and be on my own.

This day had come, and I was like a pioneer going to explore unknown lands. She wouldn't hear from me for several months. I hope she didn't worry about me, but who could blame her? The profession I'd chosen had some good qualities, but it was also dangerous in the underworld. One bad move could have serious consequences.

ON THE ROAD WITH CRAIG BICKFORD (1982)

In Columbia, I met Craig Bickford, a young, sharp kid with long hair and an average height. He was a good-looking guy with charisma and a gift of gab, so all the girls adored him. He was a talented pool player—not as good as me, but more well-rounded—a suitable dice shooter, and a great card player. He was just seventeen and drove a silver 280ZX, which I thought was cool.

After watching me play for a bit and being impressed with my game, he walked up to me and said, "Man, Cuz, you play strong; we need to go on the road." Of course, I loved the idea, and we headed over to Evansville, Indiana, to play at Ark Lanes, a bowling alley with a nice poolroom and large Brunswick Gold Crown tables.

Several bars were in town, but we planted our flag at The Busy Body Lounge. This was a strip club inside a small brick building painted white on the outside and kept very dark on the inside. Three stages lined the front of the bar, where the girls would dance, and a small pool table sat at the back of the bar.

Although this bar/strip club was small, it was very successful due to its location near a major racetrack across Kentucky's state line. Jockeys from Kentucky would come over and hang out after a race, and they usually had lots of money. They all wanted to party and gamble away their earnings. This place was like a pool shark's Disney Land for us: hot girls, booze, and gambling.

One night, we were drinking, partying, and having a great time. I started playing this jockey at the pool table for $20 a game. He was a little guy with a dark complexion, a cocky attitude, and a pocket full of money. We were playing 8-Ball, so I could stall and still win every game without him getting suspicious.

I got him down $100, and he started smarting off; his ego was twice as big as he was, and he loudly asked me to flip a quarter and call it for $100. I called "heads," flipped it, and, of course, it came up "tails," I called heads again, and to my dismay, it came up tails again! I had never been lucky at things like flipping coins that have no strategy, the thought of giving this cocky jockey my money sucked big time, but I was out of my element, so I'd treat it as a lesson learned!

At that moment, everything changed; an older flim-flam hustler named Bob came up close behind me and discreetly palmed me a quarter. I intuitively knew what this meant. The coin was two-headed. I asked the jockey to flip to reinforce my hustle, but he insisted I flip, and I called it.

I knew it was risky to give him the chance to flip, but I had been drinking and feeling reckless; it made it sure he'd keep letting me flip and call. Now I had him! It came up heads every time, and I relieved him of his cheese, which was about $1500, and the title to his car (I sold him his car back the next night for $1000).

The following day, feeling a bit hung over but elated from the night's winnings, I got dressed and went down to the end of the motel and got a Mountain Dew; I was dehydrated from the alcohol. About 30 minutes later, a knock came at the door; it was Bob. He wanted his share of the money from the coin-flipping hustle and his coin back. We shared some laughs about the jockey and how funny it was to beat him at the game he thought he liked.

"Let me get that coin back, CJ; it's a unique, perfectly balanced coin I got down in New Orleans; it cost me $250.

After pulling out 30% of the profits for his earnings, I reached into my pocket for the coins and went through them, but they all had two sides. I searched frantically around the room, under the bed, on the bathroom counter. Nothing.

Then it dawned on me. I used his $250 coin in the motel vending machine.

"Bob, you're not going to believe this, but I bought this pop with your coin in the motha fuckin soda machine!" I pretended to be upset, even though it was kinda funny, just not to Bob.

I held the can in my hand as evidence of my honesty. He didn't believe me and began getting noticeably irritated. The volume of his voice began to increase as he explained, "This handcrafted coin from New Orleans is perfectly balanced and unique! I must have it back!"

He stormed out of my room and went downstairs to the manager's office. Luckily, that was the one day of the week that the vending company removed change from the machine. Bob waited until 3:00 for this to occur and sorted through all the quarters until he found his perfectly weighted quarter. I was vindicated. Later that afternoon, I met with the jockey from the previous day, returned his title, and received my $1000.

The Busy Body Lounge became one of Craig Bickford's and my favorite places. We won a lot of money there and became friends with about five of the strippers. We made a deal with them that if they steered any of their customers to us and we beat them out of any money, they would get 20% of our take. They loved the money and partied with us, so life was sweet.

This also gave us built-in action. These girls would sit with their marks, point to us at the pool table, and say, "Look at those young boys over there; I think it's sexy when guys play pool for money. They've been losing all day. I think they may be drug dealers."

This is what we wanted them to think. We usually targeted drug dealers, pimps, bookmakers, and other underworld people because they came into the Busybody with the most money. We also told people we were drug dealers sometimes in a way that would make them jump to that conclusion; the best way to manipulate someone is for them to come up with the idea themselves, with your help, of course. I've never had anyone figure this strategy out; once they embrace an idea as their own, they will never admit they were hustled; it's because of ego more than anything.

Craig and I made a great traveling team. We walked into a small bar south of Evansville and won some money. After leaving for a while, we returned later that night when the real action was supposed to happen. You know, the big gamblers were supposed to be there. This would be the first time I had seen a mass hypnosis effect put on people and the power of linguistic programming. We knew we would return as potential hustlers, and the word would be out since we won some money earlier; they couldn't possibly prepare for what we were fixin' to do to them!

Upon entering the bar, we said we did not care about money. Craig declared to the entire room, "We had money to burn!"

With everyone's attention now securely on Craig, he reached into his pocket, pulled out a $100 bill, and set it on fire, raising it high over his head so everyone could see.

"If we cared about money, would I do this?"

Everyone's eyes were locked on the burning $100 bill, and the entire room went into a trance! They got their best shooter to play me some $50 9-Ball, and Craig went all over the room making side bets. After losing another $1500 to us, the owner of the place stopped us from gambling and said, "Listen, boys, you are more than welcome to come back and drink a few beers, but you can't play pool for money here anymore, I've got to protect my customers." We smiled and shook his hand; this was one of the greatest compliments we could receive.

Hustling the Popo in Waukegan, Illinois (1982)

I had something memorable happen in Waukegan, Illinois. I was up there with Doug Smith and Strong-Arm John, and we were at the Homestead Bar. This place was full of underworld activities and lots of big money. They had a blackjack game in the back and a lot of gambling, which drew us there. One of the main strategies we used on the road was to target bars with a lot of underworld characters, primarily drug dealers.

The Homestead Bar was known to have big bar table action in the Chicago area, and I was with Doug Smith and Strong-Arm John, two of the best. John immediately started making propositions, and they finally agreed that Boston Joey, a bar table champion, would give Doug Smith the Wild 8 Ball, playing a three thousand dollar set of 9-Ball. Another strong player there was Alley Oop. His real name was Al, and he was another bar table specialist, especially with the "big ball," back then, many bar tables used the big cue ball because it was slightly bigger than the rest of the balls and heavier.

Being heavier would trigger a diverter that would stop it from going down the same passageway as the object balls and return it through a chute on the breaking side of the table. Eventually, they put magnets in the balls to achieve the same effect, but they would be the same size and weight.

Doug went out to get his cue stick from the car; at that precise time, a line of vehicles turned to enter the place. Later, Doug joked that he thought there must have been a party coming in from another place, but it was not. He quickly realized it was a bunch of undercover police officers; they swarmed the place, making us all line up against the wall to be searched.

I was only 18 years old and had a fake ID that said I was Mike from Indiana, a real driver's license, but the picture wasn't me.

The worst part was I had a quarter bag of weed in my jacket pocket. I thought to myself, "CJ, you've got a shot. You better take it." The thought of getting locked up for the night in a Chicago jail was terrifying, but I didn't allow myself to feel anything; I had a mission to accomplish, and it was going to be a tricky one!

I had to figure out how to get rid of the pot standing directly in front of the police officer. I noticed he kept turning his head and looking down the line of us towards the front door. I crossed my arms, put my right hand inside the left side of my jacket, and reached down just a little each time he glanced to his right. I could feel the bag of weed and squeezed it as subtly as possible.

He couldn't tell I was doing it because I was moving slowly, like a predator bird fishing in a shallow stream. Again, I timed his glace to the right by removing the baggy and cupping it in my hand like a magician, putting my hands in front of my belt buckle. Again, waiting, I slipped it inside my pants and pushed it down with each subsequent glance.

Once they reached me and searched my jacket and pants pocket, no "kryptonite" was found; however, they did find my fake ID and my real ID together. The police officer knew immediately that I was underage, confiscated the fake ID, and said, "Don't come back to Lake County bars until you're old enough, kid; you're lucky you're not going to jail. You'd be popular there, and that's not good!" I solemnly agreed.

I was one of the first ones to go outside, but I didn't have the keys to the car. I looked up, and directly across the street, there was another bar. I just ran across the street and into the other bar; patrons stood in the window watching the raid occur across the street. I ordered a beer to calm my nerves; they presumed I was old enough and waited for Doug and John. I didn't have to wait long before we reunited and headed to our next spot, shaken by the night's festivities, but all in a day's work on the road where it's always a playground for the unexpected.

I was usually pretty good under pressure, and on several occasions, I outsmarted the police to hide things that would get me in trouble. There's another time I was with Big Brad from Cleveland, Ohio. He had this big orange van. We were in Milwaukee and got pulled over because we had Ohio plates.

They made me get out of the passenger side and again were going to frisk me, wanting to camouflage my vest and a special cue ball in one of the pockets. The cue balls in most bars aren't that good, for the most part. It was common practice back then for travel players to bring their cue ball and switch it into a game, which gave them an advantage because they were used to the weight and size.

When I exited the van, the police officer asked for my ID. I reached into my pocket, noticing we were parked at the top of the hill, and deliberately pushed the cue ball out of my pocket, which began to bounce down the sidewalk.

"Hey, that's my cue ball. Hold on one second. I have to get it!"

As I reached for the ball, I already had the baggie in my hand, proceeding to stuff it below my belt buckle as I'd done at the Homestead Bar in Waukegan; he'd have to be "fruity" to find it.

Trotting back toward the officer with the ball in my hand, I said, "I know it is unusual for a person to have a pool ball in their pocket, but you see, officer, I am a traveling pool player. As professionals, we carry our cue ball because the bar table balls are so bad."

This statement seemed to satisfy the officer. He chuckled, looked at my ID, and allowed Brad and me to leave without hassling us further. When I'm in those situations, it helps to act dumb and explain something silly in detail with a lot of passion, anything to confuse the situation and take their minds off thinking I'm a criminal. I always had an advantage because of looking so young, and I used it to the max; most high-school kids don't even know what playing two ends against the middle even means; in my world, it was elementary.

Playing pool has taught me to think quickly in high-pressure situations. When you're on the road, you've got to be a quick thinker because you never know what's going to come up between being robbed at gunpoint and being in a lot of these critical situations. I learned a lot hanging around some of the best hustlers in the world early in life. You can't learn that in a college classroom. Being around some of the greatest, like

Strong Arm John, Doug Smith, Omaha John, Dalton Leong, JR Weldon Rogers, and Rusty Brandmeyer.

Learning How to Win the Big Cash Endurance Matches (1983)

The first endurance player I went on the road with was Rick Thompson. He was from Saint Joseph, Missouri, and played a lot in Kansas City, but I met him in Columbia at the Columbia Billiards Center. I was sixteen when I first saw him; he had Gilligan's hat on and played barefoot. He fascinated me because he was an unusual-looking character, and he played it to the tee.

He always told me that people won't gamble with you if they think, you're smarter than they are. He went out of his way to make people think he was just dumb and called it the "Moon's Made Out of Cheese" syndrome since that's the silliest thing he could think of, but it works like a charm. Many people are looking for any reason to feel superior mentally, and we gave it to them on a silver platter! Rick Thompson's charming characteristic was his one-liners were extremely funny, and he had a dry, sometimes dark sense of humor. We used to drive through various random towns, and Rick would always say,

"CJ, look over there. This is my town. These are my people. Do you see that building over there? See that McDonalds? That's my McDonalds. Do you see that sign over there? That's my sign!" Going to Pekin, Illinois, he acted like the Pekin Owl. He put his fingers into "okay" signs, upside down over his eyes on both sides, and would make "hoo hoo hoo" sounds. He was a frickin riot, and despite his physical appearance, was super sharp and witty.

He said, "If you can convince people that the moon's made out of cheese, they will do anything you want them to do because they'll think they're superior and just won't be able to comprehend that you might be two or three moves ahead of them, they'll voluntarily fall right into your trap." I've used that a lot since then, and I've refined it as well; some of my hustling friends have seen how effective it is firsthand; the biggest suckers usually have a superiority complex; they love thinking they are superior, which is insecurity, we do something nobody in their lives have done, we encourage their egotistical behavior!

Rick loved to play long sessions, at least ten straight hours, and sometimes he would play for 30 or 40 consecutive hours barefoot. He told me you must condition yourself so that the more it hurts, the more you focus and concentrate. You put yourself into a zone and channel that pain into determination. In addition, it helps to be able to put yourself into a hypnotic trance we call "dead stroke."

He was intelligent and well-read but didn't do well in school; he was like me and probably many of us. He could see that the stuff they were teaching him in school wasn't something he would utilize except for reading, writing, and arithmetic. But you must memorize a lot of that stuff to take a test, and it may or may not be accurate. I've come to realize most of our history has been fabricated; however, at that time, it was just instinct; later, I discovered the specific details regarding the billion-dollar hustles in the world, which are rooted in us learning some bogus stuff in school.

We are all-impressionable and aren't allowed to question anything in school; after all, the "teachers know best," but the teachers have been taught the same shit they parrot to their naïve students. Rick and I liked pool school; everything we were doing and learning prepared me for multi-million-dollar business deals, something I'd utilize in Dallas.

Rick Thompson and I drove down to Dallas. I remember that when I was sixteen years old, we went to a convenience store on Harry Hines, which I later found out could be a dangerous area. Rick went into the store to get some cigarettes, and I stayed and pumped gas. This guy approached me, flashed a badge, and said, "How old are you? I need to see your ID." I told him I was 16, but I could tell I was in a bad spot!

"In Texas, you got to be seventeen to drive." I knew that wasn't true, but I was getting nervous, and he was aggressive; I could feel anxiety racing up and down my spine. Suddenly I saw the handcuffs, my heart was pounding, and he was going to handcuff me!

I jerked my head around towards the store; Rick was walking towards us. I can't imagine what this guy had in mind, but he wouldn't get those cuffs on me without a fight. I knew this child abduction stuff was happening; I'd seen all the kids on milk cartons. But I was scared; this guy wasn't a cop, but he had crazy eyes, and worse than that, he had handcuffs.

"Hey, what's going on?" The man turns slightly, showing Rick his fake badge.

"This kid was driving. He's not old enough to drive in the state of Texas, and I'm gonna have to take him to jail." My body started to coil, I didn't know if I was going to fight or be in flight, but shit was getting ready to hit the fan!

Rick knew better than to argue; he was more seasoned than me. He knew the guy was lying and probably needed money for drugs. "Can we do anything to resolve this now? Can you send him a ticket? We can pay the fine, and you'll let us go." The man's demeanor changed slightly, and Rick started talking about money, which was his language.

"Yeah, it's an $80 fine."

Rick reached in his pocket and pulled four twenty out. He knew we were getting robbed, but the penalty for resistance was way more than $80. I still remember the guy writing the ticket on a crumpled-up piece of paper. It was a total sham. I'd be robbed several times in the following years, but this was the most shameful, and if he had got those handcuffs on me? We drove to Rusty's on Northwest Highway, which was only a few miles away, and we were already stuck $80!

We pulled into the parking lot at Rusty's. It was in the same building as a strip club named Baby Dolls, and there were three other strip clubs in the same area, so there was lots of underworld activity. Rick didn't want to walk in with me, so he sent me in alone. I was still a little shaken by the robbery, but I knew that $80 was insignificant compared to what we could win in Dallas gambling at pool.

The poolroom was small; they had four nine-foot tables, a few bar tables, and a few card tables. In the following years, I'd play many gambling games at Rusty's with players like Baltimore Danny, Little Al, Lizard, John Hagger, Harley, Johnny Ross, Black Ben, and others who wanted to beat this naive, ignorant kid. At least, that's what they initially thought; some of them could never accept that a high school student hustled them with an orange lunch ticket in his back pocket. I used to do that for grins, too. We did well in Dallas, but at a country western bar off East Grand, I beat a bookmaker for $5000 while playing 6-Ball.

I remember the last trip we took. At this time, I was 18, and my street wisdom and game had improved drastically from traveling with Omaha John. We drove to Topeka, KS, to play at the Playboy Club, down to Wichita, to Burke's Steak House and a couple of action poolrooms. Rick lost every match he played. I won, but Rick liked being the player, and he was getting heavy on my shoulders.

We were going back to Saint Joseph. I was driving. He didn't even have a car, I don't think. I was taking him back to his dad's bar, and we argued most of the way. By then, I had reached a level where I could see things he was doing wrong, and he wouldn't listen to me because he was used to me being the student, not the teacher. His ego was getting to his head, and I was sick of it.

When we returned to his bar, he said, "Well, if you think you can beat me, I got $60." I still remember he had a fifty-dollar bill and a sawbuck, which we called a ten-dollar bill.

"I'll play you for a dollar a game, and you can just bust me."

I knew this wasn't about the money, this was about pride, his more than mine, but I was pissed at him, and my killer instinct kicked into high gear! We played on the bar table with a heavier cue ball because I remember my break was super good with that heavy ball. I used a 60-inch cue to break with and had the break down to a science on the small track with the mud ball.

We played for about 12 hours for a dollar a game, and I came out 60 games ahead of him; I must have had over a hundred breaks and runs. He wasn't a champion player, but guys like Mizerak and those top players could spot him on the seven-ball, so he had a strong game. I still remember he gave me the $50 and the $10, and I handed him the $50 back. "Man, I don't want your money; you need it worse than I do." He couldn't lift his head; I'd introduced him to the "feint factor!"

Losing that many games will drain anyone; it's demoralizing. That was a critical day for both of us; it prepared me for the next level I would have to reach. After that, I traveled with Strong Arm John, Doug Smith, Omaha John, Dalton Leong,

Rusty Brandmeier, and Weldon Rodgers. These are some of the greatest road players that ever lived; they had plenty of heart and knew virtually every trick in the world to win the biggest scores.

Omaha John could play 30 straight hours, but the key was to be in great shape; reverse push-ups were John's favorite for strengthening his pool stroke. He learned this from Surfer Rod, one of John's favorite road partners and a legendary hustler. Rod could do one-handed push-ups while standing on his head and betting on it. The only player stronger than Rod was maybe Mike "Tennessee Tarzan" Massey, who was also a physical beast of a man.

From age fifteen, I was heavily into martial arts and read many books about it. I would anxiously wait for the Kung Fu show to come on television weekly.

"Grasshopper, snatch the pebble from my hand. Then you may leave the monastery."

This famous line from that show indicates that Kane, the lead character, had successfully reached the level of Master and could now leave. That day with Rick Thompson, I snatched the pebble from his hand, but I'm pretty sure he felt like I broke it; these situations reminded me of the movie Highlander, where he would cut his opponent's head off to receive their energy. Our battles were less violent, but the confidence I gained from such a significant victory was priceless and carried over too many future matches.

Being on the road at my age was an accelerated course on hustling, and then I developed what I call a seventh sense for cons, deceptions, and hustle because, you know, it's just like anything else in life. When you learn it at a young age, you understand that stuff better than you could from a book, a classroom, a university, or anything else. It has become second nature, but I'll assure anyone they wouldn't want to attend some of the brutal classes I had to attend in "pool school."

UNDERWORLD ELEMENTS OF GAMBLING (1983)

Rick Thompson taught me much about what it took to be a great actor. He wasn't as he appeared to many people. But again, he was fighting demons, just like we all are. Nobody who's been in this pool world that's reached high levels hasn't been exposed to the drug world. That's true in professional football, basketball, and baseball. I know professional athletes from all those types of sports, and I was on the inside. Like NBA basketball players, I know several personally, and they all use marijuana. Back then, the NBA would allow their players to use that drug, which I think is acceptable.

The pro players told me, "You don't understand how difficult or painful it is to keep your hands above your head, guarding someone playing basketball, especially all the games they have to play. They said we can't sleep at night, it's brutal! We don't want to take opiates because they are hard on your health and physically addictive. And you know, if there is a tragedy going on in this country, its opiate addiction, not pot or weed.

Many states now allow you to grow it legally and transport it legally, but in the 80s, they used to act like it was the devil's drug that would turn you into an axe murderer or something. It was all propaganda. None of that was true; I've known hundreds of pot smokers and never saw any of them get violent. It was like medicine for us on the road, especially on the dull days when there wasn't any action.

One of the places Rick Thompson and I went to play a lot was in Tulsa, Oklahoma, at the Billiard Palace. Jim McDermott owned that place. The original location was 31st Street and Harvard. That's where I went and met Fat Randy. Man, he was another character. Mike Sigel and Larry Hubbard used to run together, and I'm not 100% sure if it was Mike or Larry that Fat Randy played. But he beat him severely and said, "Yeah, two of the best players in the world, but they can both get the eight on that bar table."

Randy reached these supernatural high levels through chemical enhancement. He chased them out of the poolroom, telling them he would give them the eight ball if they wanted to play some more. They didn't like it that night because they saw that insanely high gear! The reality was not good for Randy, though. Seasoned pros like Mike Sigel would end up robbing him on any table in the long run.

Randy was another one who struggled with his own demons, in and out of prison. I rarely was around people who shot up drugs, and there were only two people I ever saw do it. Both times, I got queasy and felt like I was going to pass out. I broke out in a cold sweat, and Randy was one of them.

We had taken a ride to another pool room, and we returned to the Tulsa Billiard Palace; he was sitting in the passenger seat and started shooting up these preludes (phenmetrazine), a type of amphetamine popular back in the '70s' and '80s. I just glanced over, and he did it. He stuck the needle in his arm and drew the blood back inside the syringe to make sure he was in his vein. When I saw that blood, I felt like I'd touched a corpse and had to jump out of the car; I felt like I was suffocating.

I have a mental phobia of needles, and I thank my mother for it. She's the one who instilled that in me. She used to tell me that when going into airport bathrooms, there were people who would try to shoot you with drugs and get you addicted. I didn't think that was true, but I believed it as a kid. But she was using negative reinforcement, and it worked because I continue to this day to have a fear of needles.

I could never give myself a shot like that in a vein. It creeps me out. Most of the people I knew who were junkies are dead now. Some made recoveries, although I think it required divine intervention, certainly a power higher than themselves. I had never been around the drug heroin either, mostly marijuana, amphetamines, and coke. I've been around groups that liked coke and partied hard, but I was fortunate and never got hooked.

One of my road partners, Weldon Rogers, told me when I was nineteen, he said, "Don't ever play pool on anything that you can put up your nose."

This was the wisdom I learned on the road from people who had learned in the streets, not in the classrooms. While in Tulsa, Rick Thompson and I played some marathon gambling matches and finally pulled out the victory; we stopped by Waffle House to recuperate some strength; we usually didn't eat when we played. We returned to our little dive motel; back then, they had a chain on the door for extra security. I was trying to slide the chain at the top, and the chain would not go in the slot. I tried and tried, frustrated. I imagined being in my "pool zone" and finally forcing the chain into the slot.

The next day, I woke up with a severe cotton mouth; I reached for my jeans and quickly put the same shirt back on. I went to the door, and my fingers searched to determine how the chain was removed. If you remember, those chains had a large and small circle at the end of a brass chain. Typically, you fit the small circle into the hole, but I somehow forced the large circle into the smaller hole. I tried for a second but couldn't get this chain undone!

Rick snickered. "You just gotta be smarter than the chain!" He went up confidently to the door, looked at it, and tried to open it, but he couldn't. We looked at each other and started laughing. I had no idea how that had happened. We had to break the chain to get out of that room. There was no other way.

I've had a couple of things like that happen in my life, and I have no earthly idea how it happened. When I'm in the zone in the pool, it's like I go from playing the game to the game playing through me; this also bridges other things. This skill enables some supernatural things to occur occasionally, but the catch is I cannot take credit for it. The ego, especially when it leads to overconfidence, blocks this level of performance, at least it does with me.

How Steve Mizerak Crushed My Basketball Career (1983)

When I was old enough to dribble, I loved to play basketball; I practiced dribbling around furniture in my house for hours and hours. This helped me develop uncanny hand-eye coordination. I'm not saying I was a great basketball player, but I created a consistent shot and was dangerous shooting from around the wing position. And from that area of the court, I was deadly. Other teams would play a box defense and put one guy on me, man to man, because I scored 17 to 20 points in games shooting from the outside, especially from the area straight out from the free-throw line.

I did love playing on our high school team, but not as much as pool, and this story is about seeing Steve Mizerak in Quincy, Illinois. He was doing an exhibition. I'd always admired Steve; I idolized him as a pool player because of the Miller Lite commercials. "Tastes great, less filling," but he would make a trick shot and say, "Even when you're just showing off," it was a great commercial.

This exhibition happened on the same night as one of my basketball games, but I decided I would instead take this "once in a lifetime" opportunity to see the living legend. I had talked to Rick Thompson, and he was stoked to go, but he wanted to get a handicap and try to gamble with "The Miz." I'm pretty sure Steve would have whipped Rick, so I'm glad we didn't get a chance to match up, but Steve gave an impressive trick shot exhibition and then signed autographs; I stood in line to get an autographed picture.

This was inspiring for me. It was awesome to meet someone at Steve's level, and he treated me with respect even though I was just a young kid he'd probably never see again. When I returned to school, the coach took me into his office, and he said, with an authentic, gruff voice, "So, CJ, what happened to you Saturday night?"

"I went to see Steve Mizerak, the professional pool player in Quincy; he's the one that does the Lite Beer from Miller commercials; he said I had a lot of talent and if I practiced a lot, I could be a pro someday!"

He didn't seem to be listening and just scoffed at me, "Yeah, good luck with that nonsense; you are off the basketball team!"

"You know, coach, I'll never be an NBA basketball player, but someday I'm going to be a professional pool player, and I'm going to beat Steve Mizerak."

I don't know where that came from; it was out of my mouth before I could pump the brakes.

Again, he looked at me like a pitiful loser and told me to leave his office. I remember going out that door and thinking, "I'm going to prove this prick wrong someday, even if it kills me!"

Less than ten years later, I played Steve Mizerak at a pro tournament on Accu-Stats at the Sands Regency Classic in Reno, Nevada. That's when I came out of my road player and hustling days; the event was my second professional tournament. The match with Mizerak went down to the very last game. We both shot world-class stats, and I ran that final rack in about a minute.

It wasn't easy, especially because one of my other childhood idols was doing the commentary—Mr. Buddy Hall is the best 9-ball player of them all! Later, Pat Fleming, who owns Accu-Stats video productions, said that match with The Miz was the best-selling video of the year for him—put that in your pipe and smoke it, Mr. Basketball coach, and thanks for the negative reinforcement. Haters do serve a purpose.

There's a difference between love and passion, you know. I love many things but am only passionate about a few. If you have anybody saying you can't do something, I will assure you if you're willing to go to the extremes chasing your dreams, anything is possible. Just put your head down and do what Steve Mizerak used to tell the world: the key to becoming the best is simple. Practice, practice, practice. I would add perfect practice is what makes perfect.

CHAPTER 2

Early Road Lessons from the Master's (1983)

I sat in the backseat, thumping through my partner's roadmap. Each state had many towns circled with names, numbers, and descriptions beside them. If I wanted more details, they also had a "spot book" with every player in each town, a description of them, and an order in which we would ideally work our way up the ladder of players and win the maximum money. We weren't interested in just beating someone playing pool; we were out to beat the whole town out of as much money as possible.

Most little towns had their "champion" that everybody would bet on, and usually, we would have to play him to win a big score, but not always. I have been a part of huge scores where we played someone who couldn't hit the ocean if they were standing on the beach. I wasn't the one who usually played the pigeons. My partner usually did that, and he looked more like a football player than a pool player, but never let looks deceive you; he could play right under championship speed, especially on the bar-size tables.

Sometimes, it wasn't easy to know what state we were in when we finally got to a hotel at the night's end, but I didn't even care. I just needed to find my next opponent like a junkie needs that next fix. I loved the action, but more importantly, I loved to win the money. Many people think they are "pool hustlers," but there are several levels that most are unaware of.

First, you have the scuffler. He is the bottom feeder and constantly moves around to different bars, looking for someone drunk or simply can't play. This type of guy wouldn't bet two big dogs could whip a little dog and usually won't even put up $100 unless he sees buzzards flying over the poor victim. Next, you have the typical hustler. This guy usually plays better than he looks and knows a thousand-and-one proposition games that look too good to be accurate but aren't. I like some of these guys, but they don't get genuine respect from my group.

Then there are the "players." These guys play like burning hell and typically don't lose any of their own money. They usually have a stake horse that puts up the money, and they play their hearts out. Unfortunately, their hearts aren't that big, and even though they play very well and run the balls correctly, when they get up against the elite group, they know their place and usually lose the money peacefully once they realize they are in a bad game.

The next group is the only one I try to get involved with, and it is purely business. I know they will get the money, and we don't have to worry about gambling, but how to milk the room for the maximum amount. We are called the "road players." We stay on the road because once people know who we are and how we play, they would rather gargle razor blades than play us for any amount.

Not only will they lose their precious money to us, but chances are they will also lose some of their manhood. I love to not only beat another player, but I like to hear that I screwed up his game for six months as a result. The beauty is that there is no physical harm, unlike a boxer who can cause brain damage physically; I just wanted to cause damage mentally and financially.

"We have arrived!" I heard as Doug pulled into the parking lot. "You better write down the names so you don't forget this time," he said sternly.

I reached over the front seat and was handed the "spot book." I thumbed through until I found the town that we were in and started to study the information. There is one main pool room and two bars where everybody gambles. The pool room had a player with a seven beside his name and a description of what he played, how much he would bet, and how he had lost the most money in the past.

The other bars had a couple of scufflers that fed off two of the regulars. One owned a car dealership, and the other was a bookmaker who took sports bets and used one of the bars as an office. I immediately knew that he would be my target. The main goal would be to go to the bar and mix with the crowd for a while. We would get on the pool table and bet a few dollars, but we would be more interested in meeting the key people and putting something in their heads that would elicit greed. You can't con an honest man. We wanted everyone to know that we had a lot of money, but not much sense.

We pulled over at a little country cafe and got some good food before we were subjected to the bar scene, where pork rinds were considered a delicacy. We would also use this time to plan and decide who would play, in what order, and if we would split up and cover the pool room and the bars simultaneously. I enjoyed this as much as I enjoyed playing sometimes because, for road players, winning is not the most crucial thing; winning the maximum amount makes the difference.

I would run into other road players who were unfortunate enough to get behind us on a road trip. They would come into town a day or two after we had left. I always got a good laugh when they would comment that we would leave nothing but tombstones in these poor pool rooms and bars.

Some of the towns wouldn't take kindly to someone asking to play for money soon after we had tortured them. They weren't in the best of moods about gambling at pool after we had drained them. After eating, we started chit-chatting with our waitress and dropping a few names that were our targets. She immediately knew one of them and began to give us personal information about him.

He will never know that he was "set up" by his friend without her even knowing it. It is amazing how often someone we meet would know one of the names on our list and unknowingly give us detailed information on where to find them and how to approach them.

Sometimes, our spot book wasn't up to date, and there would be another place to play in town or another player we could key on. It didn't matter; once we were in town for a few hours, we knew we would have all the necessary information to take off a score. This was our business, and we knew it very, very well. We got directions to where we needed to go and headed for the car.

As we drove, I noticed the snow falling and felt an instant adrenaline rush. I knew tonight everyone would be inside, out of the weather, and doing what they enjoyed most: gambling at pool. Little did they know who had just come into their little town and what was in store for the ones that would play a stranger in this game called pool.

I sat in the backseat of the car, started to rehearse my lines, and fantasized about winning my biggest score as we prepared to go to this night's office and see what our marks were willing to pay us at the chance of beating us out of our money. I grinned at myself at even the remote possibility of losing. We always walked in knowing we were the best players in any venue.

"What are we going to say we're doing in this redneck megalopolis?" I asked from the backseat, "Stop at this gas station, and I'll get a newspaper to see the local events. There's got to be something going on around here. Maybe a goat roping rodeo or a tractor race."

We pulled in, and I jumped out of the car for a newspaper. This was a standard routine before taking over the town. We would get the third degree at some point at night, and preparation was critical. If we didn't have a purpose for being in the town, it would make the locals very suspicious.

Still, on the other hand, if we convinced them that we were there for a legitimate reason (other than to hustle them out of their money), they would be easier to entice into a "friendly" pool game. We wanted our marks to think that we had plenty of money and not much sense so that their greed would get the better of them.

I opened the paper. John cracked the window, and cold air rushed inside the vehicle as I started thumbing through the entertainment section. "Here we go. There's a big farm sale at the livestock market tomorrow, and I'm sure we can get a great deal on a John Deer tractor. We can tell them that our crop just came in and we want to expand our production next year. They will think we're growing pot when we flash this wad of cash."

This was always one of our favorite ploys. We would tell people that we were there for a particular reason, but in a way that if they didn't believe us, they would jump to the conclusion that we were there to pick up or deliver some drugs. It worked perfectly because they would be trying to beat us out of our money before someone else did. Reverse psychology was nothing compared to what we were fixing to put in these poor people's minds.

"What about the tags?" Doug asked. "Yeah, I don't think they'll believe we drove 1000 miles to get a good deal on a tractor. Pull over at that hotel, and I'll "borrow" some for the night."

Once everyone knew that we wanted to gamble, someone would almost routinely check our car to see if we had out-of-state tags. We would sometimes go to a hotel and get one of the plates off another vehicle, glue magnets to the back of it, and stick them over our plates. Then, we could park in plain sight of the place's front door without worrying about spooking our potential customers.

Then, after we were done, we would return the plate to the car, and everyone would be happy. If the vehicle was gone before we returned, at least they would have one of their plates (we would pick cars that had a front and back tag). We weren't "stealing anything" but borrowing for a little while; at least, that's how we justified it.

We split up and hit the bars and the pool room simultaneously. We dropped off Strong Arm John at the pool room, and Doug and I went to the first bar. John's forte was going to a pool room, getting a game with the first guy with fancy jewelry, and losing every game for ten dollars.

This was called "laying down a lemon, "like planting seeds for Strong Arm. He knew he didn't look like a pool player and took full advantage. What would usually happen is Doug and I would end up beating all the players, and then they would all want to play John because they knew that he had lost earlier and was a weak player.

John would then refuse to play any of the players but would match up a game with the stake-horses that put the money up for the players. The players would encourage their backers to play, hoping they would win, giving them another chance. That parade was soon rained on because despite looking like a linebacker, Strong Arm was just a notch under a top-road player. By the time he started playing, we were usually big winners, and the opponent would have his "nose open" and ready to go off like a rocket.

The only time this ever backfired on us was when someone jarred Bill's drink, and we just about had to knock him out to get him to stop playing and get him out of the place. "Jar is a drug that someone can put in your drink that will put you in la la land. You will think you are playing like a world champion and lose every game until you run out of money or someone makes you quit.

I have had this happen three times, and it is no fun. I think it is used to put women in a euphoric state during labor or something funky like that. All I know is you can't quit, and you "think" you're playing well. We never did this to anyone; even pool hustlers have morals and ethics about how they operate. We operated clean hustles and would never physically harm anyone.

I liked traveling with John because getting a game was easy for him. He played the big, dumb guy routine so well that I would even start to believe it, even though I knew he was sharp as a tack. I remember one time we were hustling down in Florida, and every night, we would end up going to a late-night club for after-hours action. This place had three bars in one, but the restrooms were back beside the pool tables, and Strong Arm would ask everyone who looked like they had money to play one game for a hundred, and it was amazing how many people would take him up on it. These guys often couldn't make a ball but loved playing my muscle-bound friend.

That would never work for me because I looked like I might be a player, but John looked more like a lumberjack. That trip was very profitable because I flew in after John had already won some big money and shown his playing speed. No one knew we were together, so I played Bill in front of everyone. The first night, I lost $2800, then quit and got drunk, telling the "house detective" (the one that wants to be a big shot and tell everyone how smart he is) that I was down to make a "business deal," letting him jump to the conclusion that I was buying something costly and very illegal.

I came in the next night, and the house detective had already told everybody in town that I was a big drug-dealing sucker, and everyone started asking me to play pool. I told them I wanted to play the big guy I played last night. Just then, John came in the door. We matched up again, but he spotted the eight ball as a handicap and beat me out of another $4,200.00; I quit and had some more drinks, telling the house detective how upset I was because it looked like I was going to have to spend a few more days there.

I also told him that I was looking at a new Corvette I would probably buy the next day to give to my girlfriend. From then on, it was like shooting ducks out of a barrel. I had people calling me to make appointments to play, and of course, I knew exactly what their playing speed was. Strong Arm disappeared for a week, and I beat the area out of about thirty thousand in the next three weeks. They had never experienced anything like that, and I heard that after we left, they wouldn't play any strangers a game of pool for the next couple of months.

One thing we always did when we went to a new area was beat the small towns first before moving into the bigger cities. Through this process, we often became friends with one of the guys in a small town and talked him into "putting on a show" at one of the pool rooms in a big city. Putting on a show was what I had done with John, where you play someone just so other people can see how badly you play. You usually know the person you are doing this with because it is more like laying down a lemon if you don't.

This was especially easy to do if the guy had been hustled by one of the big city players. They would get their rocks off and pull off a score with us because they loved being part of hustling the big city "smart guys." I even had a guy refuse to take his cut because he said he had so much fun laying down the hustle that he felt he should be paying us.

Hustled by Jacksonville Harley (1983)

I've told many stories about victories, but there have also been times when I was hustled myself.

When I first met Harley from Jacksonville, Florida, I was in Dallas, TX, at a pool room called Rusty's on Northwest Highway. It was a small room but had lots of action. You never knew who would be in there at any given time. Frisco Jack often hung around there. I remember he played some one-pocket with Chicago Bugs when I was there.

This match-up was fascinating because they were both masters but had different styles. Jack was an excellent strategist; his moving ability and mind were brilliant, and Bugs, on the other hand, was a shot maker, especially with his banks. He could make just about any bank; if he didn't, he'd hang it in his pocket. It was enlightening and entertaining for me to see the contrast between their styles.

I entered Rusty's one day, and a guy was practicing alone on the corner table. A non-assuming guy, he looked like he might be a truck driver, farmer, or something like that. He sure didn't look like a pool player, so I went up to him and asked him to play, and he said,

"I know who you are. I can't play you even up," he said. I love to gamble, but you'd have to give me a significant handicap."

We negotiated back and forth and agreed to play nine-ball, but he got the six-ball as his handicap. I believe I was only nineteen years old, and the one thing about me was that I was always all in. I could never leave the pool room with money in my pocket until I beat everybody. I would line them up and play. The upside of this is I developed tremendous stamina and killer instinct. On the downside, there were a few times when I would lose all my money. And luckily, back then, there was so much gambling it was easy to get pumped back up, but nobody wanted to be broke, especially hundreds of miles from home.

So, Harley and I started playing, and it just didn't seem like the balls were rolling right for me. It just seemed like I was always in some weird predicament. Of course, I didn't realize he was a master pool hustler and was toying with me. He was playing well enough to win, and in doing that, he had me in weird, off-angle situations all the time. The balls were always where I couldn't run out, or he made a lot of combinations on the six-ball. I didn't realize it, but I had become a sucker, and I'd bitten his bait hook, line, and sinker!

I lost everything I had, about $1,200. I had jewelry, a necklace, diamond rings, and stuff I had won, and I pleaded with him to let me put the jewelry up to play another set. He shook his head and said, "Kid, I don't want your jewelry."

"Oh, just give me a chance to win my money back!" I started making my case for why he should play some more.

He motioned me over, out of earshot of the other gamblers, and said, "Listen, son. " He looked me right in the eye, and I could tell his demeanor had changed; he was no longer trying to hustle me but giving me sound advice.

And I listened. He said, "Son, you can't beat me playing this game. I know you think you can," he said, "But you can't." He said, "I won your money fair and square. But I'm not gonna take your jewelry. I've got a code that I go by, and I won't beat a man out of his jewelry or pool stick."

Then he reached into his pocket and said, "I know you don't have any money, and you probably don't want to ask," but here's $100. Please go to your hotel room and sleep because tomorrow's another day. Come back tomorrow, and you'll find a way to get pumped up again."

Begrudgingly, I put my cue stick away, returned to my hotel, and slept. The next day, I had breakfast and returned to the pool room; I only had $60. I started playing with a guy for $20 a game and ended up beating him. And then I played another guy, some $100 sets, and turned my stack into $500. And before I knew it, or they knew it, I was up to about $1,600.

The guy I was playing finally lost enough and quit. I hadn't noticed him before but looked at the bar, just slightly out of view from the table. Harley was beaming at me with a smile. I put my hand over my chest, which meant "thanks," and nodded at him; he just looked at me and winked—that was all the communication we needed. Those of us in the hustling game can almost read each other's thoughts.

Harley taught me that I'm never going to be the most intelligent guy in the room, and maybe not the most brilliant guy at the table, but I can recognize when things aren't right, and I have the knowledge and willpower not to play. I had to dodge many hustling bullets, and situations like the one with Harley have come up many times since then. He saved me a lot of money from that lesson. There's a lot of wisdom in those pool rooms, especially when dealing with people who understand the art of the hustle.

How to Outsmart the Bandits (1984)

Weldon Rogers, also known as Junior Rogers, was the best one-handed player I've ever seen. I met Junior in a bar in Marion, Indiana, when I was with Chuck Bradley, another road partner with whom I had won a lot of money. He wasn't a great pool player, but he was great at stirring up action and a triple brutal fighter; sometimes, that's a plus when playing in dangerous places. Weldon told Chuck he was there to gamble, and we matched up a game he played one-handed, and I got to use two.

I thought, "How hard could it be to beat someone who played one-handed," but something in my gut told me this was too good to be true. I gave him the six, eight, and the break on a bar table. That's a big spot. However, I could beat him at the level I was playing; he would have a lot of pressure on that one hand.

But after just a short time, probably fifteen minutes, I went over to Chuck, who was observing thoughtfully from the sideline. "Man, there's something about this guy. I don't know if I can beat him. I've never seen anybody play one-handed this well; it's freaky, and he's got to be somebody!"

He made balls effortlessly by resting the cue on the side of the table and could lift the cue up, "jacked up," and draw the ball back. He could do anything I could do two-handedly, apparently.

"I don't think I can beat him!"

Looking somewhat irritated, Chuck said, "Well, I guess you better figure it out then, don't be a wussy, you gotta put some pressure on his ass!" That's what it's like when you're gambling at a high level. You often must figure out how to detect weaknesses to beat your opponent, which takes sophisticated observation skills and creativity. But I was in a serious trap.

As I sat there watching him make shot after shot, I thought, what can I do two-handed that this guy can't do one-handed? Then, suddenly, it dawned on me. He can't jump balls one-handed. We played two-shot push-out back then, where you roll out any time, so there was no kicking. It's how everyone played; gamblers would not play one foul "Texas Express Rules." Hardcore gamblers would laugh at tournament players who wanted to play those rules, saying, "I'm not kicking at my money. Are you silly or stupid?"

Nowadays, people don't even realize that the two-foul game is superior to what people currently use. So, I had my strategy and changed my game plan; I started rolling out to set myself up for jump shots. He let me shoot them, and I would jump over the ball, make it, and run out the table. When I did this, I knew he could not jump, which was something even this seasoned hustler hadn't considered. I beat him out of $2,200 that night, and he was visibly upset; he wasn't used to being outsmarted, especially by a kid.

Ultimately, Junior and I became great friends, and it worked out well for him because I was supposed to play him again the next day, but I smelled a hustle. I asked my friend Chuck to call him and make an excuse not to show up, "Tell him my dad died or something, and I had to leave town."

Unfortunately for my friend Doug Smith, he thought his game was stronger than mine and played Weldon the same way, except Weldon stipulated there would be no "jump shots" allowed. He started playing better, and losing that money to me set him up to win the big money, ending up a $12,000 winner against Doug. He told me later that he ended up winning a little over $50,000 the next month because every time he matched up games from that point on, it was with the stipulation that you couldn't jump the balls. Nobody could win like that, but he told everyone who would listen that an eighteen-year-old kid had beaten him.

A few months later, I was traveling in North Carolina with Omaha John, one of the best undercover players in the country.

We went to this bootleg joint in the middle of nowhere by the Pee Dee River, a few miles from Albemarle, NC. A guy named Sharkey was the target there. He owned the place and was, come to find out, a very dangerous man. He was a gentleman to gamble with as long as he wasn't drinking; I gave him the Wild 6 Ball, won a few thousand, then the Wild 5, and dusted him off for a little over $6000.

A few days later, Omaha John went home to see his wife and a little girl; we had been on the road for a month, which seems longer when you're doing what we were! I stayed in the area and went back to Sharky's place. I was out at a picnic table with some guys, drinking a beer and having a little "enhancement" (what we call getting high).

It was getting dark, and a lone streetlight lit the area. We heard a rustling noise in the trees to my left side. Out of the woods came a stick-up man with a nylon over his face. As a rule, I kept only a few hundred dollars in my pant pocket, but that night, I had $5,200 in case Sharkey wanted a chance to get his money back. When I saw the man come out of the woods, I slipped $5000 under my leg and tossed the $200 on the picnic table.

"That's all my money!" I said as I tossed the money; the gunman was behind me and pushed the gun in my ribs.

"That can't be all of it; stand up!" My heart was pounding as I got to my feet. The man took my wallet out of my back pocket, and when he saw it didn't have money, he threw it on the ground. Fortunately, a car came up the gravel road heading towards the river where some houses were located. The robber said, "Anyone move, I'll blow your fuckin heads off!"

I had my hand on my money clip; when he turned back into the trees for cover, I jumped off the picnic table and dashed for the door, zigzagging. My mind was racing, and I could almost feel the bullet going through my back from the angry gunman, but no shot came.

Shaking from adrenaline, I ran into the bar and shouted at the bartender. "Give me the gun!" in an elevated voice. He said, "What gun?"

"We just got robbed; I know you have a gun. Give it to me!" He reached beside the cash register and pulled out a loaded .38 pistol.

I raced out the door and ducked behind a brick barbecue pit they cooked on occasionally. I fired over the picnic table three times into the woods, not hitting anything but making sure the robber knew he wasn't the only one with a gun and I was willing to shoot! Just in case he decides to return to finish the job. It may not have been smart, but in emergencies, I trust my reflexes and responses; they have saved my life on several occasions.

The next day, the police came, which was awkward because I was using the name Mike and saying I was from Nebraska even though my license said I was from Marion, Indiana. I went by the name Mike, but using the "CJ" name wasn't smart; it was becoming well known. Later, I found out that Sharkey didn't like to lose money and was triple treacherous. That night, he drank more than usual, took some pills, and passed out on the couch, which sat near the wall of this small shack, thus providing himself with a solid alibi. I saw through it, though; he was the one that had me robbed, and that's why the gunman knew I had more money; it was a miracle he didn't get it!

After hearing of Sharkey's exploits and lack of honor, I targeted him with an elaborate hustle and called my good friend Junior Weldon. After telling him my plan, he drove down from Indiana and said we would put the re-rob on him to teach him a lesson. I went back into Sharkey's with no indication I knew what he did and played for two days like nothing ever happened.

Weldon came in after the second day, and we pretended to match up like two strangers meeting for the first time. I beat him even, spotted him the seven, then gave him the six, seven, eight, and the break with him playing one-handed and "won" $1000 from him, giving Sharkey his $500; the trap was set! Weldon pulled out his large cash roll to flash it openly, making Sharkey lick his chops because he could tell Weldon couldn't beat him. I called it a night and announced I would head to Charlotte for a few days to see what action I could round up.

Seeing how easy it was for me to beat this one-handed player, Sharkey propositioned Weldon for some similar action. Over three days, Weldon beat Sharkey out of $12,000 while I relocated to a new hotel room, waiting for half of the hustle. We knew Weldon was in potential danger of getting robbed, so when they were supposed to play on the 4th day, Weldon never showed up.

Sharkey had got the "re-rob" put on him; it couldn't have happened to a more likable guy! Later, I found out he was suspected of killing his ex-girlfriend, or she shot herself in the back of the head with a shotgun. I returned several times after that; I must have had a guardian angel watching out for me. I was no stranger to life-threatening situations, but sometimes, I took crazy risks that put me in some awkward situations.

THE NORTH CAROLINA HUSTLE (1984)

North Carolina was known to have some of the best pool players and gamblers in the country back in the 70s and 80s. As a road player, you had to be advanced to go to North Carolina and make money because they would put you to the test. There were a lot of high rollers and lots of players. I was in Eastern North Carolina, going by the name Mike Hulse. I had my glasses on and usually had some disguise to throw people off so they didn't think I was a pool player. I carried my money in my wallet, like an average Joe, rather than a hustler's bankroll, and wore cowboy boots.

There was a pool room there where the owner gambled pretty high. I'd been in there two or three times, just playing and breaking even and losing a little bit of money, flashing money, so I had a story that made people believe I could gamble high if I wanted to. I had just been robbed at Sharky's place, so I was a little bit leery about carrying a lot of money.

I would flash my wallet full of cash and then keep the bulk of my stash back in the hotel room. This went on for several days until I had the owner and other players convinced I was an easy score. On this day, I had left most of my money at the hotel and only had a little over $1,000, which I thought would be enough because I wasn't ready to unload the big guns yet.

I'm now like a local in this place and had the owner set up – ready for the kill. He's the one I had targeted, and I convinced him I don't play that well. As fate would have it, a pool player named Pete Horn came in with two of the biggest high rollers in the area. Pete Horn was a good player and was known never to quit. You could win big if you got him down and he had the right people backing him.

I saw this as a golden opportunity. He asked around, and people told him I gambled and didn't play well. He walked up and offered me the seven-ball if I wanted to play. Of course, I didn't have much money, but this is a potential $20,000 or $30,000 score." And my hotel was about 50 miles away, so I couldn't go back and get my money.

I pulled the owner aside and said, "Let me talk to you for a minute." We retreated to his office, and he said, "What's up?"

I said, "Listen, I'm an excellent player, and that Pete Horn just offered me the seven ball with Plowboy and Hooker backing him, they might lose $50,000. I can beat him even, but I don't want to play him for a small amount. If you back me, I'll split the money with you, and I guarantee I'll beat him, and we may win a big score."

The bar owner hesitated for a minute, then started laughing hysterically. He said, "What? I don't know what you're smoking, boy, but you need to smoke more of it or quit entirely," because I've seen you play, and you're not that impressive."

I said, "Yeah, but I'm hustling you guys. I'm a lot better than what you think I am, better than what I appear; I'm one of the best undercover players in the country!"

He just laughed and didn't believe me at all. I went out and ended up passing up the game. It was brutal because I really could have won probably $20,000. I returned to the same place a couple of days later, but this time, I had $5000 on me. I matched up with the owner, and he was still laughing about me, saying he would beat this young "professional pool hustler." But he wasn't laughing for long because I spotted him with the eight, seven, and six, winning almost $7000 for that night's work.

After it was over, he didn't look so comical. He came up to pay me the last of what he owed, "You were telling the truth, weren't you? I can't believe I was so stupid!" He couldn't be mad because I'd told him the truth; it reminded me of the saying, "It's easier to hustle a man than convince him he's been hustled."

My Best Undercover Names (1984)

Back when I was traveling all over the country, I was with many advanced road players, and the one critical thing back then was there weren't cell phones and the internet where people could get a picture of you or put something on a forum to get you outed. The main thing you had to do was change your name. So, I used a variety of names. One was Mike from Indiana, another was Butch from Tennessee, and I also went by Chris from Missouri.

I had to be more careful in Missouri because, knowing I was from there, people might recognize me. On this day, I was Butch from Tennessee when I went to Morristown, Tennessee, which is east of Knoxville. There was a gentleman there, Frank Seals, who owned a pool room and was a big gambler. He was a successful businessman, very cash-flush, so he would test your heart!

I went in and caught him in a different pool room downtown. I told him I was Butch, and, of course, he had a few interrogation questions for me to answer, but I passed all his tests. I matched up with him and gave him the six-ball and the break, playing 9-ball. I got ahead of him and gave him the five and the break, still playing 9-ball. After a few more racks and me running the table, I gave him the game I knew he couldn't resist: the five, seven, and the break, playing 9-ball. We played for about 12 hours. Like I said, he put you to the test. I ended up beating him out of

$16,000. Not only was Frank not upset, but he took a liking to me.

I had a 25-foot Pace Arrow motorhome that I was driving around. He gave me permission to park beside his pool room, plug into his electricity, and gave me a key to his pool room so I could come and go as I pleased. His pool room became a real hot action spot. There were some great players, like Shannon Dalton, who was only twelve or thirteen years old at the time, but boy, he could play, especially the strategic game of One-Pocket. He beat all the adult players, and it was amazing for a young kid to be as talented as he was.

His dad was with him most of the time, greatly influencing him. Weldon and I had gone to their hometown of Somerset, Kentucky, and beat them out of almost $10,000. Our strategy was simple: I'd play Shannon and lose a couple hundred, then play his dad and win a couple thousand. Weldon matched up with Gerald, getting eight matches to three in a One-Pocket game, and Weldon played one-handed. They ended up playing eight to seven after several matchups.

Shannon could see what was happening and ended up telling his dad, "If you play this man again, you're just a sucker; he's playing you like a radio!" Weldon moved like a ghost; not only did we get the money every time we gambled, but we also made them like us. I became good friends with Shannon; we teamed up several times, and years later, he was on my Mosconi Cup team when I was the player captain. I ran the last rack with Earl Strickland as my partner. That rack was some of the most intense pressure I'd felt, partly because we were in London and especially because Earl was my partner; if I'd dogged it, he would never let me forget.

NOW OR NEVER MOMENT (1984)

Omaha John was one of my most outstanding mentors in my teenage years. We met in Omaha at a huge pool room named 'Big John's,' which wasn't named after Omaha John, even though many people thought it was. Of course, he was the best player there and one of the most outstanding bar table players in the United States. David Matlock was considered the best. However, several players like Buddy Hall, Keith McCready, Earl Strickland, Larry Hubbart, and unknown players like Vernon Elliot and Fat Randy from Tulsa could win on a bar table.

Omaha John was one of the best bar table players in the country; David Matlock tried to spot John the "Call 8" and lost $60,000. He had an oil man named Dugan backing him, so many road players went to Oklahoma to play, but few won the money gambling with David "The Giant Killer" Matlock. There were a few other excellent bar box gamblers, but Omaha John was feared. He knew how to win the money!

When I was a teenager, we took several trips together; on one of our most successful ones, we ended up in South Carolina, in a little town called Bishopville. The bar owner was known to play anybody with the five ball and the break, playing 6-Ball. This handicap means he gets to break every time, and he wins with the five or the six. That was his standard game against road players.

We didn't have to hustle the guy; we heard he could be dangerous. He had put a gun on some other road players and taken back his money when he figured out that he got trapped. We declared ourselves road players immediately, and while John talked to him, I examined the pool tables. The place was small, but it had three Valley Bar Tables in decent shape; I could see by the white lines on the table where the owner liked to break from. The break in 6-Ball isn't that big of a spot because the balls won't find a pocket like they do in 9-Ball unless they know the trick break, which I could tell this man didn't by the 'evidence" on his table.

John wanted me to play first and act like the stake horse or money man, so we might get two separate games with him if I won first; many times, they would play John to try to get even. The issue I'd been having was closing my opponents out; three different times on that trip, I'd get a thousand or two ahead of my opponent, then have mental lapses, and they would come back and get all the money back. I would get ahead of my opponents and couldn't knock them out. I kept getting ahead a few thousand, then let up, and they'd get even and quit.

We weren't making the money that John needed; he had a family at home, and I didn't, so not winning wasn't such a big deal to me, but he was in a different situation. I was gambling like I didn't have any heart, which is the ability to close out your opponent, stick the knife in, and twist it, is how a lot of hustlers described it. Killer instinct is essential when you're a gambler, especially a road player. You've got to have a lot of heart because you've got to be able to win against the best players in the country and be willing to play marathon matches and crush their will at the drop of a hat!

Anyway, I started playing the owner the 6-Ball game and got ahead of him again. We started raising the bet, and I got about $2000 up—then, suddenly, I just couldn't run out. My concentration wasn't good, and things were bothering me; I could hear people talking, another guy eating potato chips was bothering me, and I was a mental mess! John approached me and said, "Listen, we've got to make money out here. I'm not on the road for my health. You either turn this around so we can start taking off the bigger scores, or I will return to Omaha. You can fly wherever you want to go!"

His stern tone and the thought of failing hit me hard. I leaned my cue against a chair, took a break, and headed to the bathroom to give myself a "pep talk," and it better be a serious one to stop the anxiety I was feeling. I walked into the tiny bathroom, locked the door, and looked at myself in the mirror, directly in my eyes, "It's now or never, CJ. If you're going to be a winner, you've got to do it now!"

It seemed like a positive force came into my mind, a moment of clarity; I went out, picked up my cue like a sword, and my entire attitude changed. I stopped shooting low-percentage shots, stopped spinning the ball so much, and started hitting that dead ball as John did, you know, that touch of inside that makes the cueball float from position to position like it's on a string.

My game just clicked. I got in a zone—we call it a dead stroke—and ran over the guy. We raised the bet again and ended up beating him out of $8,600; it looked like the blood had been drained from his face. As I put my cue away, the guy is leaning against a bar stool with his head down—he's steaming! Suddenly, the guy jumps up and runs at us. We ran, too, sprinting to the back of the bar and out the exit door. I didn't know what he would do, but one critical issue was John's car; it had been acting up!

It was a diesel, and it took several tries to start earlier; it seemed like the battery might be messed up. When we got out of the door, it was pouring rain. We raced for the car as fast as we could and looked at each other as we thought the same thing at the same time: Will the car start?

We jumped in the car, and John jammed the key in the ignition. He glanced over at me and smiled, and the diesel engine roared to life. I don't know what we would have done if it hadn't started. We were blessed on the road through our adventures, and this was a prime example.

More than just winning and getting out with the cash, that experience was when I made a turning point, proving to myself I had the heart I needed to reach my full potential. The caliber of pool I would have to play for the next few years to survive would be challenging. I'll never forget what Omaha John did for me:

tough love. Sometimes, you must have people tell you it's now or never, and I'll be forever thankful for John saying what had to be said at precisely the right time! The game was becoming my teacher.

When I was in Morristown, Omaha, John called me and told me a funny story about a tournament in Tupelo, Mississippi. He was at a table with three other pool players he didn't know, but their conversation interested him because they were arguing over who was the best young player in the county.

The first guy said, "I think it's Butch from Tennessee. He came through my town and gave me the Wild 7 Ball; he ran out from everywhere but the bathroom stall!"

The next guy states, "I think it's this kid from Indiana named Mike; he came through my town and beat everyone!" He gave me the six ball." which is more of a handicap, "And beat me like a drum!"

The third guy says, "Oh no, you are both wrong! A kid named CJ can beat all of them. He came through my town and gave me the freakin five ball, playing 9-ball, he never missed a ball!"

Omaha John couldn't control his laughter, so he stood up and made a beeline for the bathroom because I'd used all three names on the road. I guess I'm the best young player in the country, especially if the other two I'm competing with are me." We got a kick out of that for months!

Turning Lemons into Lemonade in Atlanta (1984)

After Omaha John and I split up the money in Bishopville; We worked through South Carolina, hitting every bar and pool hall we could find. After that tour, we had pumped up our cash to about $17,000 each. Omaha John went home for a while to see his family, and I went to Atlanta to visit my childhood friend, John Emerick, who was now attending Georgia Tech. I missed my old high school buddy and reminisced about our time together playing tennis and our adventures on the road.

I was also going to Atlanta to recoup; I was burned out on pool. My weight had dropped to about 140 pounds, whereas when I was playing my best pool, I was around 172 pounds. The weight loss clearly showed that I needed to take a break. The long nights, partying, and poor diet had begun to have an apparent effect on my overall health. All I had been doing was playing pool. I was eating, drinking, and thinking about it from when I awoke in the morning until I finally called it a night. Sometimes, after twenty-hour sessions.

I took it to the extreme: you must push yourself to reach higher levels. I used to joke about liking pain; in my chosen profession, you had to face and deal with pain. I was always prepared to gamble until I dropped, literally! What I was learning to do was put myself in a trance; we call it the zone or the slang "Dead Stroke." At that time, my passion for doing whatever it took to improve overrode my pain, but right then, I needed a nice, long break.

When I went to Atlanta, I quit playing pool for about a month. I didn't play at all and just played tennis with my friend, John. I just took it easy, partied, and made friends. Atlanta had gorgeous women, and fortunately, many were around BJ's Sports bar, where businessmen played 8-Ball routinely for $100 and $200 a game; I was scouting places but not trying to gamble, just drinking and trying to get laid.

When I decided to start playing pool again, I went to this little bar in Marietta, Georgia, and asked around. I hadn't been playing pool, but I still had a lot of money, about $10,000 in cash. I beat a few locals, and then they got Randy Randalls to play me. He was a pretty good player around there, but he wasn't supposed to be able to beat me. I started playing him, and we're playing for about $50 a game. I'm stalling around, and the game goes to $100. Now, I've got him in a position to take the whole room down. I've got my girl, Zia, taking side bets; now all I gotta do is what I do best. Run out!

The problem was I couldn't come out of the stall. That's one of the dangers of stalling, which means playing under your skill level to entice people to bet more. When you're a pool hustler, it's essential to do that well, but there are times when you can't come out of it, and that was one of those times. Randy Randalls dances around the table and beats me out of about $1700. And I was like, "Oh my God." I was riding home and just so angry at myself, thinking, "How did you do that?"

Then, about halfway home, it hit me. Man, this is the perfect lemon. I didn't do it on purpose, but losing that money, I knew everybody would find out about it, and now I could get into a lot of action. There were a lot of good players around Atlanta, and I proceeded to play all of them. Some of those guys, like Eugene Browning and Robert Turner, gave me the seven ball, and I worked my way up the ladder playing in the pool rooms daily and the bars at night.

There was a high roller named Mean Dean there backing the best gamblers. Mean Dean had quite the reputation of being a gangster. The little kids in the area used to tell Mean Dean stories around the campfires to scare each other; that's how well-known he was. And I beat Mean Dean out of quite a bit of money. I'm still probably lucky something terrible didn't happen to me, but he always liked me, even though it was a love-hate relationship. He respected me because I beat everybody without saying a word, and, more importantly, I bet my money as much as possible. One night, Dean cornered me at a bar I'd been gambling at and said, "You lost to Randy Randalls on purpose, didn't you?"

I kept calm, looking into Dean's cold, piercing blue eyes, knowing he'd suddenly stopped many hearts, and mine was beating irregularly. "Yeah, Dean, just so I could trap you, Sir." Dean hesitated and cracked a sly smile.

Chew, from Raleigh, NC, told me he was riding with Dean to an action spot; it was a five-hour drive, and three hours into it,

Dean looked over at Chew and said, "You know what it's like to kill a man?" Chew told him no. Fortunately, he didn't.

Then Chew looked over and said, "You're not thinking about killing me, are you Dean?" Chew said he was poised to grab the steering wheel and jerk it as hard as possible. He is a big, tough man. Dean smiled, "No, son, I like you." Dean said nothing else for an hour; Chew said that was the most extended hour he'd ever spent in a car. That's what I enjoyed about the underworld in Pool. There were lots of characters, but only a few were dangerous, and for some reason, those guys usually liked me. The key is how we carry ourselves; I always treat them respectfully and with healthy caution.

On the Road with a Jewel named Zia (1984)

While hustling pool, I used to create three different scenarios while traveling. I would travel with other players, high-dollar gamblers, or sometimes with men who had other areas of expertise, usually card or dice players. Another scenario was traveling with attractive women, which gave me a distinct advantage. Playing and reading the room correctly is impossible. To maximize profit, it's vital to have someone who can take the "rail" action; often, the player isn't the one with the most money to lose. I've made some of my biggest scores on the rail, taking side bets.

Hot females who know how to hustle can get men who are usually scared to gamble. Besides, there's nothing better for a man's confidence than having the sexiest girl in the room on his arm. Social status is important, and when you've seen winning thousands of dollars in a night off older men, it can be an aphrodisiac to beautiful women!

Zia and I were having some drinks at a place called The Saint, a nifty little nightclub near downtown Atlanta. "What do you think about taking a long vacation, going on the road, and traveling around the country for a few weeks?"

Zia took a drink from her Vodka glass and looked at me from the corner of her eye. "Like in that pool movie you made me watch?" she smiled, knowing full well she enjoyed every minute of 'The Hustler' with Paul Newman and Jacky Gleason.

"Yes, but hopefully, our show will have a better ending!" she smiled as she scratched my calf with her high-heeled shoe. She knew how her looks affected men, and I attracted her mainly because I treated her like an obnoxious little sister half the time. She couldn't figure out which had a magnetic effect.

We packed up all our stuff—there wasn't much—so I rented a new Lincoln Continental from Budget. I could get the car for under $200, fully insured, weekly. I liked renting vehicles on road trips because I could usually get the tags I wanted and would choose plates strategically to match the area I was gambling in. Someone would usually check cars for out-of-state identification in big action spots.

I had a red, white, and blue pool soft-sided pool case that made me look like a sucker, and I used to spray-paint my pool cues black. Even a Balabushka cue I had was spray-painted black. It wasn't even a good black color. I'd put it on a little too thick, and it started peeling off. It looked like it had some billiard leprosy, and people would make fun of my cue. This was all part of the illusion I tried to portray as being a weak pool player.

We would do two different hustles when I was with Zia. I wore this hat with two pigs having sex that said, "Making Bacon." I combined it with a pair of Wolverine boots and a camouflage jacket. I wanted to appear like a country bumpkin, ready to lose my money. Most professional pool players dressed sharply, so I was trying to create a mismatch, especially since I looked so young. We would enter a pool room right after it opened and march straight up to the guy behind the bar.

I'd say, "I'm really good. Is anybody as good as me?"

He'd look at me like, "What do you mean?"

I repeat it, "I'm really good. Is anybody as good as me?"

With an inquisitive look, "You mean at pool?"

I said, "Yeah, that pool game," and pointed to a pool table.

He said, "Well, there's nobody in here, so nobody's as good as you."

I turned to Zia, saying, "I told you; nobody was as good as me." And we'd turn around and head for the door. Well, they never let me get to the door.

"Hey, kid, do you want to gamble playing pool?"

And I'd stop with her, pause for a couple of seconds, turn around, and say, "Well, yeah, but nobody's as good as me, so I'll bet $20 bucks on an 8-ball game."

"Well, I think some guys might be as good as you. If you play for $20 a game, I can call them, but they like to play 9-Ball."

I agreed to that reluctantly, of course. He would call somebody, and they'd be down there within ten or fifteen minutes. Of course, I'd stall with them, get the bet up, and win their money. Zia would be over there, just flirting, smiling at the guys on the side, and trying to get a "sweat bet." It worked well, plus they could never get mad because I told them nobody was as good as me. It pays to be honest!

The other thing we did was I'd send Zia into a pool room I knew had a lot of gambling, and she'd play pool by herself. Pretty soon, these guys would talk to her, and she'd act like she was upset. She'd say, "No, I'm waiting for my boyfriend, but he's in a poker game and always loses. If he loses again, I'm just going to leave him." The guys would start thinking that I was a sucker. When I did come in, she would say, "Did you lose again?"

And I'd say, "No, I won this time," and show a bankroll of what looked like a lot of money. Sometimes, it was disguised because, being that young, I didn't want to carry too much money because there was a chance of getting robbed, so I'd wrap a bunch of $20s with a couple hundred and usually pay and collect from my wallet. It never failed. These guys would get up there trying to beat me, fantasizing about winning her; imagine that! They were like shooting ducks out of a barrel; they had no idea we were sophisticated hustlers.

I ran that hustle with her many times, but as relationships go, it ran its course; maybe she finally figured me out, and we parted ways. I took her back to Atlanta, went on my way, and forgot about her over time. Fast forward eight years later, and I was at a tournament in Chicago. The word was out that I would be there because I was beginning to be on the tournament posters, and there was a lot of publicity about me. Zia found out that I was in Chicago, where she had gone to live. She got a hold of me, and I said, "Why don't you come down here to the tournament, and we'll hang out?"

She came down to the tournament, and we went to the bar, had a few drinks, and reminisced about old times because we were still on good terms. After a few drinks, I asked, "Do you want to see my fish collection?" I'd ask her about it when we met at BJ's many years ago. I used the same line, and she laughed, "I'd rather sit on you and watch the fish get jealous!"

We went to my hotel room and were still talking and catching up on the time we had spent apart. As we entered my room, she asked, "So, how old are you now?"

I said, "I'm twenty-seven."

And she says, "Oh, yeah, OK. That sounds right. I'm twenty-five."

I hesitated for a moment, and I was like, "Twenty-five? That doesn't make any sense. I said, "When we met, I was nineteen, and you were twenty-three." I asked, "How did you get younger than me?"

She explained, "Oh, there's something I never told you. When I was down in Atlanta, I had a fake ID that said I was Zia and was 23, so I could get in the bars because I was only 18."

I was shocked, "Oh, man, are you fuckin serious? You've got to go!"

"What do you mean, what's wrong?"

I couldn't conceal the irritation in my voice, "You lied to me about your age, and I probably don't even know your real name." It didn't even matter at that point because, as a hustler, you never wanted to be hustled, especially by your road partner. It hit me hard after she left. I was a little upset, to tell you the truth. Not because she gave me the wrong name and was younger than me, but because, at 25, she looked even better; I should have at least had sex with her a couple of times before I kicked her out. Live and learn!

Zen Master & Pool Hustler, Dalton Leong (1983/84)

Dalton Leong was originally from San Francisco. His ethnicity was Chinese, although he could pass himself off as Japanese or Spanish, and he even told them at one point he was an Eskimo. He had a thin frame, around five feet seven inches, and black hair. His forearms stood out most; they were ripped, and when he played pool, the veins made him look like a pool-playing Bruce Lee.

He was an accomplished actor who starred in an episode of Ironsides and a few other notable movies and plays. He also wrote poetry, practiced tai chi and martial arts, and was extremely well-read, sophisticated, and deeply spiritual, especially as a pool hustler.

Dalton knew so much more about the game than I did then, as I was only seventeen when we played and traveled together. Even though he was an accomplished, intelligent, seasoned player, that didn't help his eye issues. He wore glasses when we met and had contacts, but his eyes dried out when wearing them in the smoke-filled pool rooms.

Dalton played Wild 8 Ball under champion players like Buddy Hall and Earl Strickland. This means he wins on the eight or nine ball, and his opponent only wins on the nine ball. This handicap is heavy when they make the eight ball on the break or combination shots. It's about a 15% advantage on average, which may not matter when playing the world's greatest players.

We met in St. Louis at Afton Billiards. I was playing all around the St. Louis area, and the OK Corral pool room was on my rotation of rooms. Dalton was with a tall, country-looking white guy; they immediately seemed to mismatch. When we started gambling, I could tell he was a seasoned player, which was unusual at that time in America; the only Asian champion player traveling the roads was Hawaiian Brian, who I later found out was one of Dalton's road partners. Brian had a pool room in Honolulu called Hawaiian Brians. He also mentored Rodney Morris from the islands, who won the US Open and was one of my most formidable opponents.

We matched up a nine-ball game for $30 a rack and went back and forth for several hours. I could see flashes of brilliance, but he kept missing key shots. I knew something was bothering him but couldn't tell what it was; later, I discovered he had eye issues.

I was intrigued and decided to get to know this man better. We sat down out of earshot and started leveling with each other about who we were, how we gambled with various players and our short-term plans. Our life stories crisscrossed each other with similarities, and I felt a deep kinship and liking for this mysterious road player. After some time, Dalton asks, "Hey, what do you think about us taking a road trip together?" I agreed quickly, feeling I may learn much more than pool from this gentleman.

We decided to drive up to Minnesota; Dalton received a tip on where to play in trade from another pool hustler who wanted to know where to make money in Texas and Southern Louisiana, where Dalton had taken off some big scores. This is how our underground network operated; we traded spots with other road agents, including the towns, pool rooms, and names and descriptions of the gamblers; this information was worth tens of thousands in the right hands.

Trying not to make a name for ourselves, road players generally work the smaller towns first, then move on to the bigger cities where the real money is. By the time we reached Minneapolis, we had managed to pump over $20,000. However, Dalton had trouble with his game; he had some problems with astigmatism in his right eye and found it challenging to focus in low light, and the smoke irritated his visual situation.

This gave him obvious physical challenges, but his mental game was off, too; 90% of the mental game is confidence, and it's impossible to be confident when the balls are fuzzy. As a result, I was banking most of the money, which was okay with me. I wanted to play anyway. I remember we were at Gentleman Jim's, a 24-hour place in Minneapolis, and he played a guy we'll call TW, a big, tough guy.

Locals in the bar said he had to run 10 miles a night to get to sleep, with stories about him snapping the butt of a cue in half when he got angry for losing. We never dodged anyone just because they had a bad reputation; as long as they put up the money, there weren't usually any altercations. He wouldn't match up with me but saw Dalton as someone he could beat.

Dalton and TW put up $3500 apiece on the light above the table. This was common practice in those days because everyone watching could see if anyone reached up on the light, so it was the safest place; I've probably put over a hundred thousand on the light myself throughout my career. They were playing the first one to 15 for the four thousand, and it went back and forth at first, but then Dalton caught a gear and was ahead 14 to 10. Dalton made another great shot and ran down to the nine ball; I held my breath watching the last shot because Dalton had been dogging a lot of money balls.

Not this time; Dalton fired the last ball in, and suddenly, TW jumped off his bar stool, ran up to the table, reached up, and grabbed all the money! He looked at Dalton, who had moved over in my vicinity, almost in a protective position.

"You aren't getting this money tonight!

The last time some road players beat me, they left town and didn't give me a chance to get my money back." "I'm going to play you tomorrow for $5,000, but you're not getting this money, I remember a vein protruding from his temple as he glared at Dalton. For an instant, I visualized Dalton doing a spinning dragon kick and dropping this tush hog in his tracks.

Instead, Dalton stepped towards him and calmly said, "I understand how you feel. It's not cool to beat a man and quit him, winner, but you'll give me my $3500 back; that's my money, not yours. TW paused for what seemed like a minute; his eyes were dilated. He might not have been on drugs, but he sure looked like it to me. On the other hand, Dalton was dead calm; I thought he wasn't scared and even looked comfortable.

TW took the $3500 and tossed it toward Dalton, but he didn't move at all. I quickly bent down and picked up the money. Dalton held his position, his eyes never leaving the man. He was wise; keeping your composure and position under pressure is best, especially in dangerous situations.

The next day, we went back to Gentleman Jims. It was a 24-hour pool room off Lake Street, so we usually were there after midnight, but Dalton had told TW he'd meet him there at 4 pm. About five minutes after walking in the door, a pimp named Little Richard came up and said, "Your man can't play today, but not because he doesn't want to, he's in jail. After he had left the pool room, he stopped off and robbed a drugstore; the police got his description and arrested him a couple of hours ago. He was locked up, and the judge won't make bail yet; this was armed robbery. He probably won't be out for a while!"

I couldn't believe what I heard and slammed the palm of my hand on the bar; what a horrible roll this was! Looking to my right, on the other side of Richard, was Dalton, sitting at the bar, taking a sip from a cup of coffee. "Did you hear that?" I exclaimed, "This takes the cake out of all the excuses I'd heard!"

Dalton smiled, "CJ, my boy, remember what I told you? Money must always be a result, not the incentive; as far as I'm concerned, I won a lot more than money in that session; I won back my confidence, and that's priceless to me right now!"

Dalton put me through a rigorous training schedule, culminating in my requirement to run five racks in a row consistently, every day with the break and first shot playing 9-ball. He used to say, "Concentration and focus aren't mastered by trying hard; this pursuit is counterproductive. When we try hard to focus and concentrate, we become just another person trying to focus and concentrate, like a drowning man trying to swim against the current. Focus and concentration come from connecting and absorbing ourselves completely into what we do and let the game flow gracefully."

When the player performs "in the flow," they transform into an instrument of the game, which needs to express itself through the player. I feel a transformation from playing the game to the game playing through me. Dalton urged me to feel like I became the cueball, not looking where I wanted to go as much as I felt it floating from position to position like it was on a string and I was the puppeteer.

Gentleman Jims was also the first place I got robbed at gunpoint. I was with Dalton at another pool room across town where I'd beat a drug dealer out of $2700; we immediately drove back to Jim's and parked his van around the corner. He entered the pool room, and I stayed outside to polish off a little weed Dalton had given me earlier; fortunately, he took the keys. When I locked the van and started to go around the corner to the pool room, two guys came around from the opposite direction, rushed me, put me up against the van, and stuck a gun to my throat. They demanded my money and wanted the keys to get into the van.

Fortunately, I didn't have them; the gunman stuck the pistol even harder into my throat, and I was up on my tip toes against the van. I was white as a ghost, but they could tell I didn't have the keys. So, they took my cash out of my pocket and took my cue stick, which was my worst loss because it was my beloved Bob Rundy Sneaky Pete.

I'd been running five racks in a row for a month with this stick – it was part of me, like an extension of my hand, and I loved that cue. I still had five $100 bills in my back left pocket that they didn't get, but I'd seen my life flash before my eyes as the streetlight reflected off the pistol barrel. The two robbers high-tailed it around the van and were gone, leaving me stunned, frozen in time for what seemed like minutes.

I ended up running back into the pool room; they said my facial color was green, and I shouted, "I'd been robbed." Some of the guys ran outside, but they were gone. I knew that stick would never return, but I wasn't thinking about that as much as how close I had come to death. Getting stuck up at gunpoint makes playing pool for a lot of money seem easy; the three times I would be robbed at gunpoint made me mentally stronger, especially in high-stress situations.

I asked Dalton, "What will I do without my stick?" Dalton barely looked up, sipping his cup of coffee, "You can use my old Meucci cue – you have five racks to run tomorrow."

We're always going to have good and bad things happen. The good part is that we won a lot of money up there. The bad parts were that I got robbed, he got stiffed, and then, on the way out of town, we were driving his Volkswagen van, and suddenly, in the back, it started to smoke. I yelled and called it to his attention, and he pulled over.

This was just in time because the entire undercarriage and engine caught fire. We got as much of our stuff out as we could. It wasn't complicated for me because I just had things I'd taken on the road with me, but he had a lot of personal items that ended up going up in flames. He wrote poetry in most of his diaries and notes and had a lot of sentimental stuff; he lost everything except for a few essentials.

We ended up on the side of the road. Someone was nice enough to pick us up, and we drove south. I could see in the rear-view mirror the smoke going up; the van was blazing and looked like a hundred feet tall; it all happened so fast; it was intense! Life happens fast sometimes. Dalton used to say, "Preparation is all, readiness is everything," but some things don't give us the time to prepare, and we were not ready.

Dalton was quiet, processing what had just happened. I knew it was devastating to him, but he never showed any emotion or brought up the incident. We talked about it briefly, but Dalton had already accepted his loss; he reminisced about some of the private diaries he had, more to himself than to me, and then I remember he quickly wiped a tear from his eye; we never discussed it again.

THE CORPORATIONS (1984)

A natural thing happens when there's a big action spot, and a lot of money passes back and forth. You know, life-changing money. It'll attract the best hustlers. What they'll end up doing is forming a corporation. It's not a corporation that takes lawyers to draw up or anything like that. This is a corporation that's not even a handshake agreement. The participants know what the deal is. They only want to know what percentage of the money they get and who the targets are.

One of these places, called The Rack, was in Detroit. They had a corporation up there with seven different people, and they all got 10%. If you were going to play with one of the big-money guys up there, you had to give up 10% to each. So, you would end up with 30%. The house ranged between some of the guys, who were 5% guys, and there were 10% guys, which meant the house got 10% of the gross winnings.

I played a guy named Cletus and beat him out of about $18,000 one night. He was a 10% guy, and there's another guy they called Jew Paul and another guy, Rosenbaum, who ended up losing over $15,000,000 over just a few years. Supposedly, Rosy flew weapons for the government down to Columbia in South America and then flew the "empty" planes back to Detroit; they must have paid him well to lose 15 million. Everyone in the corporation became millionaires.

One of the other things that I did quite a bit was find out who was in these corporations at these big city pool rooms and go in with a plan to beat them all. Sometimes, they'd bet all their money on one person, but I generally would want to start with the weakest guy in the group, trap him, and then figure out how to get the corporation to bet all their money on a single player, usually the best player. They're not going to lose all their money on the weaker links of the chain, so to speak. To win the biggest scores, you either must outsmart them or outplay them; I found it easiest to give them the best of the game and win anyway. We call this outrunning the nuts.

Some of the guys I traveled with were experts in this area: Strong Arm John, Dalton Leon, and Rusty Brandmeyer. Of course, Omaha John and Big Brad from Cleveland, Ohio, knew how to maneuver a room, and some had skills that were better than mine. They may not have played as well, but having the ability to get good games is a rare talent. Even when you develop the skills as a pool player like I did, you still must get the money and learn to take action.

When you get in a position around one of those corporations, people ask me, what do you do? The main thing is when you're around a group of hustlers, never say yes to anything. Always say no and then try to figure out the best play. Then, you decide what game you will play that gives you the most significant advantage. This may take a few days, but the time can pay off handsomely.

The best way to get information from these guys is to go around and buddy up to them and ask them questions, knowing that pretty much everything they tell you is going to be misinformation or a flat-out lie because they're not in with you; they're in with their group of players. You will always have an X on your back, and that's another thing that I look for in these different pool room situations. Whoever has the most money has the most oversized X on their back, so once I figure out who that is, I look at the hustlers around them and know their agenda.

I get a lot of information without relying on anyone to tell me the truth because it's not their nature to help a potential target. People pass on information whether they lie or tell the truth; in the high-dollar gambling world, we are trained to look at both sides of any situation, calculating risk, reward, percentages, and whether the information may be a double or even triple steer. The standard double steer is when someone goes in with you to play a gambling match and is actually in with the other player. I've had that happen and outrun the situation by going into a trance and playing at a level they didn't count on. We call this outrunning the nuts.

Not so much anymore, myself, because I'm not into that lifestyle, but it's good to know how to defend yourself against con artists and political hustlers who are profiled on TV. Just like martial arts, I didn't learn martial arts to be able to beat people up. I learned martial arts to protect myself, others, and friends. My thirst for knowledge has always had positive side effects, like studying communication, which has always interested me.

When I received my degree in neurolinguistic programming, it wasn't to program others' minds, even though I've used some advertising and marketing techniques that had indirect commands for my Dallas businesses. When I learned the structure of language better, some of the road players I'd been around impressed me even more. They didn't learn their skills in a classroom; they learned them in pool rooms and gambling situations.

Every time I watch the news, which is rare, I think about being back in Detroit: everybody's playing a role, and they're telling misinformation and lies. There are probably some genuine, honest, trustworthy people. Still, coming from the hustler world, even when I got into the nightclub and restaurant business in Dallas, I found my competition treacherous; the people lacked honor and integrity. The opponents were even more cunning than the gambling hustling business, which was odd. But I could maneuver around and do well because I had that road player seasoning; I had tricks up my sleeve that they had no way of knowing.

Being streetwise is, I think, a necessity these days; sometimes people are too book-smart, you know, and they're caught in a box. They can't get out of it. And these days, the main thing when you're up against the greatest hustlers is never to go with them. Always wait. Always say no. Get more information.

Realize that what they tell you is probably misdirection, so formulate your beliefs, ideas, and plans based on that knowledge and always be aware. Our gut instincts are very powerful, and I trust my instincts, especially when I'm playing pool or evaluating sophisticated hustles; there isn't anything new under the sun, just the price tags for advanced cons can be in the billions. I've studied ones that brought in trillions right under everyone's noses, but that's another story.

THE RACK, DETROIT, MICHIGAN (1984)

When I was nineteen years old, I traveled around the country, looking for action, and the place I'd heard a pool player could become a millionaire was in Detroit. I landed in Detroit with twenty-three hundred bucks in my pocket and $2500 in jewelry. One of the hotspots for high-stakes gambling was a place called The Rack, a private gambling club. It was located on 9 Mile Road, where you had to press a buzzer to enter the front door and another buzzer to enter the pool room. They protected the place because hundreds of thousands of dollars were there at any given time, and millions passed through hands, sometimes weekly.

They had barred one man who would call up there every day to cuss whoever answered out until they hung up, so they would put the phone in a drawer, and every minute or so, they'd open the drawer, and the guy was still cussing them at the top of his lungs. I never asked, but I was curious what the circumstances were. I'm sure it wasn't an ordinary situation; nothing at The Rack was ordinary!

I played for a bit, left, and returned, only to stay up too long and lose all my money on the first day to a guy named Johnny Ross from Jacksonville, Florida. He was a notorious pool hustler, sharp guy, and great grifter; he played cards and pool at a high level and was gifted at getting people to play and go for the maximum amount of money. He convinced me to give him the eight-ball playing 9-ball and eventually beat me out of all my money; he was clever; he always waited until I'd been up over 24 hours; he knew my weakness and exploited it like a cat with a mouse.

That night at The Rack was ugly; my wrist started twisting on me, I was a mess, the pool player lifestyle could break me down at times, and I'd been drinking and partying too much, playing marathons, and making some bad decisions. These were phases I'd go through; it almost seemed like I was punishing myself. My pain threshold was always high, but I wasn't born with it; my life seemed to draw it in and hit me over the head with it; maybe I was just masochistic.

I returned to my hotel room, put my jewelry away, and decided to go next door to get some breakfast. After eating, I returned to the room and went to sleep. When I got up, I looked in the drawer where I had my jewelry, and it was gone. So, when I went to eat breakfast and returned, I guess a maid or somebody with a key stole all my jewelry.

Now, I have no money or jewelry, and I had to call home to get my mother to wire me $500, which my mother was nice enough to send me. I felt defeated, which was a low point in my pool career, but looking back, it's the training I needed to get tougher; even a sword must be beaten on to have a sharp edge.

With my $500 in hand from Western Union, a guy I met at the Rack told me to go down to this little bar, where the guy that owned it was a sucker, but he had one gimmicky thing that he liked to do: he wanted to play people who used this stick that didn't have a tip or ferrule. Nobody said this pool hustling business would be normal by any stretch of the imagination. I drove down, parked in front of this little, white building with a sign that said Open, took a deep breath and entered the bar. It was a small place with four guys drinking around a horseshoe bar.

I approached the bartender, ordered a Budweiser, and sat down a few seats from the locals. "I'm really good. Is anybody as good as me?" I told one of the men who seemed to be catching a good buzz.

The men stopped talking, looking me up and down, "Good at what?" I pointed at the pool table, "That pool game over there,"

One said, "The owner will play you if you use the stick." The others laughed, "Yeah, get the stick, get the stick!" They began chanting in a unified rhythm.

The bartender reached above the bar and pulled down this house cue stick with no ferrule or tip. It was only the stub of a dowel at the end; for a second, I didn't know if it was possible to play with. Right about that time, the door opened, and a man with a beard and flannel shirt stepped in. I immediately suspected he was the owner.

"Hey, this guy wants to play you with the stick." They all chimed in together.

I was like, "Oh, wait, wait, wait. I'm not going to play with that thing. That's crazy. It doesn't have a tip, and it doesn't have a ferrule."

The owner said, "Are you looking for action?" And I said, "Yeah, I like to play. I'm really good."

And he says, "I love to gamble, but you're going to have to use that stick."

I quickly responded, "Well, I can't play without a tip; that's crazy!"

The owner said, "Well, I'll give you a handicap playing 9-ball." We bantered back and forth, and then I agreed to him giving me the six-ball playing for $50 per game.

I played well with that stick and kept grinding it on the floor to roughen the wood and grip the ball better. Each time I broke, pieces of the stick would fall off, so I was just worried about running out of wood before we were finished. I beat him unmercifully because I'd already got the line that he wouldn't quit, and I needed the money. Within four hours, I spanked him for 20 games, which was $1000.

Naturally, when it was time to settle, he informed me he had no cash. My heart sank, but I did my best not to show emotion. "Hey, if you want to ride to my house, I'll get you your money."

I'm thinking, "Oh, boy, what's going to go wrong now?" I was already so down on myself, but I thought, "What do I have to lose at this point? The man owned the bar, and I hadn't heard anything negative about him other than he was a degenerate gambler."

He took me to his house, came out with 20 brand-new $50 bills, gave them to me, and I was off to the races. I got in my car and pointed it straight back to The Rack to see if I could turn the wood I had just won into a lumberyard. When I returned to the Rack, I started practicing because you were allowed to practice for free.

They didn't charge you for any pool time. However, if you gambled with any of the corporate guys there, you had to give up a percentage of your winnings. There were some 5% guys and some 10% guys. And really, it's gauged on how much they would lose; the big high rollers were 10% men, and they were all capable of losing over a hundred grand in one night.

Johnny Ross approached me while I was practicing and motioned me over.

"Hey, kid, we got a game for you that you can play against this guy named Cletus."

When he said "we," I knew already that this was a gambling game set up and backed by the Rack's corporation. I've been around enough that I could tell if a pool room had a corporation, and it would only take me a few days to figure out who the members were. It's such a significant advantage when you have hustlers together because they can double steer other people into their partners, and they would never know; they can also give up false lines about their partners. They can win money in many treacherous ways, and you can't do that if you're in there alone. Getting in with the corporation stationed at The Rack was a positive thing. It was like being sponsored by the mob but without the frills, thrills, and secret oaths.

I usually traveled with at least one other person and often two other hustler friends. We could do similar things but not nearly as well as those with a pool room staked out. Detroit had so much action; there was a corporation with seven different players, and I knew who a few of them were. It took me a few days to figure out who they were, but I did eventually.

I knew Johnny Ross was part of it, so when he said "we," I knew what he was talking about. And when he told me that I could get 30%, I figured that the other seven partners got 10% apiece. So, based on the percentage alone, I knew how many people were in this group. Regular people will never know that this is happening, and if they stuck their noses in any of the gambling, you could rest assured they'd end up broke; only exceptional players could go against the Detroit corporation.

Johnny, who reminded me of a used car salesman, whispered loudly with his hand cupped to the side of his mouth, "You know, we're going to put up all the money and give you 30% when you win." I resisted that slightly, and I knew that was the deal. But he said there's a catch. "You're going to play this guy named Cletus, and he won't play you unless you insult him.

I mean, you gotta talk dirty to him." Johnny continued, "You have to insult this guy, you know, call him a dirty son of bitch, and no good piece of shit pool player, blah, blah, blah."

I cringed, making a face like I'd bit into a sour lemon, "Are you kidding me?" That's just bizarre, and I thought playing earlier with no tip or ferrule would be the most unusual event of the day. I heard the buzzer at the door, and in walked this huge guy. My heart skipped a beat because I knew this monster would probably be my target. What had I gotten myself into?

He must have been at least 6 foot 4 or 6 foot 5 and looked like Brutus from the Popeye and Brutus cartoon. He had a stocky build and a three-day beard that he probably grew in about three hours. He was a menacing-looking character, and I thought, "Oh my God. I got to talk nasty to this guy." I felt like suddenly the room had turned into a movie set; all I had to do was act the part.

Johnny gave me the sign, and I was motioned over. Johnny went up to him and said, "Cletus, you are a big, ugly piece of crap. I didn't know they let your kind in the front door. I figured you had to go in the back door with the rest of the garbage."

That's how it started. Johnny motioned to me, "We got a kid over here that wants to play you. Some of us think you're scared of letting a kid beat you." He immediately looks at me and says, "Oh my god, you look like the kid brother of a 16-year-old girl I used to date."

I followed suit, cussed him out a bit, and told him everything I could think of, trying to insult him into action. He finally had enough nasty banter and agreed to do some gambling, and we started playing One-Pocket. The object of the One-Pocket is that you can only score if balls are put into the corner pocket at each opposing foot end of the table; both players have one pocket in which they can make balls. If a ball goes into any other pocket, it doesn't count, and if you scratch, it is a foul and should result in spotting a ball as a penalty; if you don't have one, you'll owe the first one in your pocket.

I gave him nine to four. In other words, I had to make nine balls in one pocket, and he had to make four balls in his pocket, plus his scratches didn't count. That means he could foul any time and wasn't punished. We played for $900 a game starting and, after an hour, raised it to $1800 a game, which lasted another three hours, and I'd beat him out of $18,000 when the smoke cleared. My suspicions were correct, and trusting Johnny Ross proved a good move; I had the nuts in the game, even though that's a huge handicap, and I hadn't had much One-Pocket experience at that stage of my career.

He paid off all the money and said a few other nasty things before he left and walked out the door. Johnny and I went back and divided up the money. I got 30%, and the corporation got 70% after we paid the house $1800.

I said, "Man, Johnny, that guy was just freakin' weird."

And Johnny replied, "Yeah, guess what he is going to do now, which is what he does every time he loses."

"What's that?"

Johnny said, "He is going to get a limo and hire three hookers. He's going to have them tie him up. One of them will put a loaded gun to his head, and the other two will whip him with wet washcloths, and they'll drive him around Detroit like he's been kidnapped. That's what he likes to do.

When the smoke cleared that day, I had about $5800. I went from being utterly broke to having almost $6000 in my pocket, which was a huge stress relief. I hung out at the Rack for a couple of weeks and met one of the colorful characters in the history of pool named Cornbread Red. He was an older man —I mean, looking back, he wasn't that old, but as a young guy myself, he still played well. I used to pester him to play Nine-Ball, but he wouldn't play that game. He wanted to play One-Pocket, and I didn't feel like I could move strategically with him; he had too much knowledge. So, we just became friends; I got a kick out of him. He always had a smile and a big wad of chewing tobacco in his mouth; he'd laugh, spit, and cut up with lots of pool slang.

One of the things I used to make fun of—was his slip stroke. And when I said, "Make fun," it was ribbing him because this slip stroke was one of the most potent strokes I've ever seen in pool. If you don't know what a slip stroke is, it's when you hold the cue up near the front of the wrap, and then as you're drawing the cue back, you slide your hand back almost to the back of the cue and then go through it.

It's a motion that generates an incredible amount of power. Back then, the tablecloth was slower, and you had to have a better stroke. Cornbread could rip that cue ball. He always used to impress me; I loved watching him play. They played One-Pocket on a snooker table for ten, twenty, and even fifty thousand a game, which was something to be seen. Guys like Bugs, Grady Matthews, Sammy Jones, James Christopher, Jack Cooney, and various colorful characters were there.

Cornbread told me one night one of the funniest stories I've heard. He said he went into this bar and was supposed to play this "Tush Hog," which is usually a big, tough guy, you know, that's intimidating. He was told to go in there and play this guy. He enters the bar, looks around, sees him at the bar, and heads in his direction.

Cornbread marches up to him, taps him on the shoulder, and says, "Hey, buddy, what's your best game?" And the guy, having a bad day or something, turned around and said, "Fighting is my best game," and just hauled off and smacked Cornbread, knocking him clear across the room up against the wall.

Cornbread slid down the wall, almost completely knocked out, landing on his backside. He shook it off, seeing stars, got back up, looked back over at that guy, marched right back up to him, tapped him on the shoulder, and said, "Hey, buddy, what's your second-best game?"

This big guy turned around and said, nine ball is my next best game! Cornbread said he matched up with him, made a few hundred dollars, shook the guy's hand, bought him a few beers, and left with the money. That's what the real road players could do—get the money and make them like it; this was one of Cornbread's best games.

After leaving Detroit, I went to South Dakota and got to the finals of a big tournament at the Corner Pocket pool hall. Scott Kito beat me in the finals. He was a seasoned player, and I still made careless mistakes; tournament winners don't usually make unforced errors. But my game continued to improve; the next chapter would be in South Carolina and Florida, the Sunshine State, where there was lots of gambling in the winter months when the drug dealers and bookmakers came down to escape the cold, northern weather.

CHAPTER 3

BATTLING THE COLUMBIANS FOR BIG MONEY IN MIAMI, FLORIDA (1985)

I lived a year and a half in Tampa but spent much time in Miami. I was there for a couple of weeks and got to know this Cuban guy named Freeman. We hung out in one pool room off SW 6th Street in the Cuban area. He steered me into some games against Colombian drug dealers; the Cubans and Columbians had a kind of rivalry. One night in the poolroom, Freeman called me over and said, "Listen, kid, I got a guy here in Miami that's got significant money, and he's willing to bet high on this guy. They're flying in from South America."

"Really, who is the player?" I asked curiously.

"It doesn't matter. He's probably a great player, but we've been watching you; we think you can beat just about anybody right now. Don't worry about the money; we'll stake you as high as they are willing to bet!"

I met Freeman the following evening, and we drove over to this big, gated community. He pushed some buttons, the front gate opened, and we entered something that looked like another world. I mean, these houses were immaculate—massive, palatial estates. We pulled up in front of one that was especially impressive. It looked like a white palace and reminded me of a Capital building with carvings and massive columns; it was like stepping into the Scarface movie.

We rang the doorbell, and a large, well-dressed man opened the door. We stepped into the house and followed the man down a long hallway into an impressive game room. It looked like the table was carved out of one piece of wood on top of a wooden lion; I remember it had a lion's head, and the four legs were like a giant lion's paws. I don't know what kind of table it was, and I couldn't imagine how much it cost. A Latin guy was practicing, and I knew he was their player. He had a fluid stroke and looked like a very accomplished player.

I watched him practice for a while. Freeman was like, "What do you think?"

"I can beat this guy. I already saw his weakness, and I can exploit it. Make sure you bet as much as possible once I give you the signal," said I, putting my hand over the center of my chest. We played the first set, raced to ten for $10,000, and I remember it was 8 to 8, and this guy had a critical shot. Tough cut shot - shoots it, makes it, goes back and forth down the table, kisses off another ball, and scratches.

I got the ball in hand and completed the rack. Then I broke and ran the last rack to win the $10,000. If you remember the show, the main bettor looked like Ricardo Montalban from the T.V. series Fantasy Island. He wore a white suit with a black tie, touted a small mustache, and was a sophisticated-looking man.

He begins, "Let's get it out of the dirt. What do you say we bet $10,000 a game?" Freeman looked at me, and I gave him a hand over the chest, which means green light in the pool world.

"You got action!" We flipped the coin, I won the toss, and I won five racks in a row on him. He made a ball, and I couldn't get out, but I wedged him between two balls. He kicked at it but didn't hit it, so I ran three more racks off. We went back and forth for a while, and then I ended up closing out with another four in a row, winning 12 games at $10,000. We ended up winning $130,000. Of course, that wasn't my cut, but I did well.

As we were leaving, Freeman went out to get his car, and the guy said, "Hey, kid, come here. I want to congratulate you." I go up to him, and he shakes my hand. I can feel him give me a piece of paper. I went out the door and slipped the paper into my pocket. And, of course, we're happy and celebrating; we drive back to the pool room, stopped by my car, and Freemen takes five rather large stacks of cash, puts them in my trunk, closes the trunk, and goes into the pool room.

We had a couple of victory drinks and celebrated a little bit. But as I was leaving, I returned, sat in my car, and had to think about that piece of paper. I reached in, got it out, unfolded it, and it said, "If you want to make some serious money, give me a call," and had a phone number on it. I was like, "Oh God, I have a feeling about what this is about," and my hands started trembling. I remember getting that paper out several times, staring at it, emptying my mind, and waiting for a sign – it didn't come, so I never dialed the number.

Adventures at the Doll House in Fort Lauderdale, Florida (1985)

Strong Arm John and I tortured all those unfortunate players around Fort Lauderdale, West Palm, and Miami; we heard about some excellent action in the Keys, so John and I headed south. We won a sizable amount of cheese in this neighborhood bar known for its high-stakes gambling among the local players. We arrived in the afternoon; Strong Arm made a beeline to the bar and asked if anybody gambled. They immediately said Billy Bob, claiming, "He's never been beaten!"

John and I looked at each other, forcing back a smile, and inquired when Billy Bob usually comes in. They said that he arrives between 7:00 and 8:00 every night. They said that he had never been beaten the second time; John and I locked eyes for a moment as if reading each other's minds. "He has never been beaten yet!"

We returned just before 7:30 and scoped out the place. It was a long room with a bar on one end and three Valley bar tables lined up to the back wall. There were just a few players, but the bar was packed, which was a good sign for side action. The door opened, and a man who looked like a sailor, with Popeye-style tattoos on his forearms, walked in.

John headed towards the door and stopped Billy Bob with a big smile and exaggerated body language; John could sell an Eskimo a snow cone, and his track record matching me up was almost a hundred percent. John motioned me over, and we started playing him for $10 a game. The locals didn't realize that Billy had never been beaten because he also never played any strong players; he knew all the best players from Florida. But I was just a kid, not much of a threat to someone who had "never been beaten."

"How much are we betting on the side?" I whispered to John when he came back from taking his side bets.

"Like $640 a game." I tried not to show the emotion I felt inside, but something seemed too good to be true. Was Billy Bob a threat to win? After a couple of shots, I could tell he wasn't my caliber, but there was still a danger of the guy having a great night. Fortunately, it wasn't Billy Bob's night; we won all of Billy's money and every dollar in the bar; even the owner and bartender were betting and lost all the money in the cash register. We cleaned out the entire place, and I guess they will be talking about that kid who finally beat Billy Bob for years to come, a kid named Mike with a musclebound friend named John.

The second time I went to Florida was with Chuck Bradley, my buddy. Chuck had an Airbrush Magic van with a big Airbrush Magic logo on the side, and we told everybody that we were down there making T-shirts and airbrushing, which I didn't know anything about—just enough to fake it. Fortunately, people didn't ask questions about the specifics of airbrushing and T-shirt making.

Chuck told me, "You know, we're going to get a lot of action, but there's one guy in particular that I want you to beat. This is personal." The last time he matched up against him, he beat his player and did some underhanded things that Chuck couldn't forget.

There was a place called the Dollhouse in Fort Lauderdale, which was a famous strip club. If you remember the Dollhouse in Fort Lauderdale from Motley Crew, released in the 80s, there are even some other songs about it. We tracked down the player; he owned a local pool room, and Chuck found out he had a crush on one of the strippers. He found out who it was, and we went into the Dollhouse. He tracked down the girl named Trish and made a deal with her. The next day, when I went in and got a game with the player (I'm not going to mention his name), we played, and I was stalling with the guy trying to get his confidence up.

Then we put up $2000 to play a set. And, of course, Chuck was making the game, and he already knew the guy. At that time, he still thought Chuck was a sucker. So, I started playing the $2000 set, and that girl from the Dollhouse came in. She comes up, waves at the guy, then goes right over to Chuck and gives him a hug and a kiss on the lips. Chuck takes her by the hand to the other side of the pool room, and they sit and start talking and laughing. She's flirting with him like they were on their honeymoon.

The guy was crushed. He lost his concentration, and I beat him out of the $2000. You could have fried a potato on his head;

he was so hot that he went outside and did doughnuts for thirty seconds. We went outside, and there was black smoke and the smell of burnt rubber in the air. Chuck thought that that was the funniest thing. Not only did he get to know that girl, but he took her back to Indiana, and I think she stayed with him and his wife for about six months.

It turned into a short-term relationship, but I heard later that the two women ironically ran off together, but he didn't care; getting girls was second nature to him. We had some good times; I still can't believe Chuck's nerves; he had balls of steel and got me into a lot of games, and I think my record with him was spotless. He always gave me a lot of confidence in harsh, dangerous places because he was an excellent fighter. I once asked him what to do if a fight broke out, and he said, "Just keep 'em off my back, and I'll whip the entire bar!" and I had no doubt that he could!

Hustling Kentucky with a Call Girl (1986)

Kentucky was a tremendous pool-hustling state, with many gamblers and serious players in the small towns. They would put you to the test. If you were going to go in there and try to beat them, you better be prepared to battle until they said uncle because they wouldn't quit easily; they were full of heart. I had just beaten Gary Spaeth up in Cincinnati when I came down to Kentucky; I was with my girlfriend from Florida; she was a real character with jet-black hair and seductive blue eyes.

Sandy was mesmerizingly attractive, and I found out later that they recognized me because of her, which was a huge knock. It was always hard to pinpoint me because I changed my appearance regularly, and it's hard to describe me. But it was a lot easier when I was with this girl because the rumors quickly circulated about this kid traveling around, who plays high-level pool. They also described my girl, and that's the information that was tipping everyone off and ruining my action games.

I played with this guy in one of those small-town pool rooms close to Corbin, Kentucky. All the pool rooms back then had a payphone. I was playing this guy, hustling him, and setting him up to win some pretty good money, but that's when the phone rang. Somebody answered it and called my opponent to get on the phone. He talked on the phone for a minute, looked at me, and returned, and after that game, he quit and acted funny about it.

Then I went to Lexington, looking for action at Danny's All-Star Billiards. I was in his place, and the same thing happened. I'm playing this guy, and the phone rang. They called him up on the phone, and he talked. When he returned to the table, I could tell he had that look on his face. I asked him if he wanted to finish the game or quit now. He smiled, said he'd finish the game, and he did, and then he stopped, unscrewing his cue. "You're too good for me." I was thinking, "Man, this is brutal."

We went to a few other places, and I went to a town up in the mountains to hunt down this outstanding player, who worked on the railroad and would gamble high. I went in with Sandy, and the setting was perfect. It was snowing lightly, so all the gamblers were in the pool room. It was the ideal stage to win some serious money. We started out playing for $10 a game. He was hustling me, which was perfect because I was hustling him. He raised the bet to $20, then to $50, we raised it to $100, then to $200, and by the time the smoke cleared, I beat him out of over $6000.

As we were leaving, the payphone on the wall rang. I told Sandy, "Hold on for a second," and went over to the payphone, picked it up, and said, "You're too late!" Sandy smiled and said, "We're starting to get ahead of the knockers, but it won't get any easier." She was right. I decided to head south. Alabama and Mississippi had some players I'd been meaning to sneak up on, and they would have no idea they were on my list, like a wanted poster in the hands of a bounty hunter in the Old West. We made our rounds and returned to Tampa; another relationship had run its course, and I was ready to partner up with another talented road player.

BATTLING MATLOCK WITH "BOOM BOOM," BILLY JOHNSON (1986)

One of my partners, who was ideal for me, was Junior Weldon Rogers. We looked similar, and he always passed himself off as my rich uncle, who liked to bet on me. We went around the country and won a lot of money together, and we wanted to do some serious gambling against the world's greatest players. We decided to attend a tournament in

Alabama; everybody that was anybody was there: Buddy Hall, Keith McCready, Earl Strickland, Allen Hopkins, Nick Varner, and on and on. It was a big action bar table tournament, and side betting was everywhere.

I was with Weldon and a guy named Berle Gabbard from Corbin, Kentucky, who steered me around a lot up there. We also met a friend from Michigan named Oscar, who had a large bankroll and wanted to put me into action. He wanted me to play David Matlock, the best bar table player in the country.

Naturally, I wouldn't have wanted to play him heads-up, but Weldon said that the corporation would back me and that they'd bet on the game if Wade Crane, AKA Billy Johnson, could break for me. Now, Wade was known to have one of the most powerful breaks, if not the most potent break, in the country. They called him "Boom Boom" because of his break.

Weldon had played several people with Wade, breaking for him in the past and won. There's a bit of a trick when somebody is breaking for you; it doesn't necessarily matter if they break better than you. It allows them to perfect their break and gives you the mindset to run the table every time because you're not distracted by the need to focus on breaking, and that helps, especially when my partner had a superior break than mine.

Weldon ended up matching up the game with Matlock and me. We were betting $10,000 and a significant amount on the side. I was nervous but still playing well and was very confident in every aspect of my game. I'd been playing a lot, and Wade had been playing primarily on nine-foot tables, but we played on a bar table during these games. He was struggling with his timing and having trouble with his break.

We went back and forth, and I got seven games ahead, and then Matlock ran eight in a row on me. I'm trying not to get rattled, but Wade, sitting over there with me, was wholly stoic and had a powerful presence. He kept saying the right things to keep me level-headed. After Matlock ran those eight racks, Wade said, "Listen, kid, I'm ready to get this break working. And when I do, we'll beat him 30 ahead, if he doesn't quit."

I saw the fire in his eyes; they seemed to be blazing. For some reason, I completely believed that what he said was true! I felt a synergistic confidence with Wade on my side! A couple more games went by, and we traded rack for rack and remained dead even. Then, Wade gets up to break; his demeanor changes and you can feel it. He hits the cue ball with such tremendous power that the cue ball goes up in the air about 2 feet and bounces down right in the center of the table, with the balls fighting to get in the pockets.

He made four balls, and I was straight in on the one-ball, and I quickly ran out. His break had become unstoppable, and it had a powerful effect because when he got that break working, I also got the running out part on a string and fired everything in the back of the pocket. Within a short period, we began beating Matlock and went up ten racks ahead without David getting many shots. Weldon looked around the room and said, "Anyone else can get the handicap of the last two!!" This meant that if they played, they would never have to make the nine-ball. This was more of a psychological spot, but it did have some value.

Wade was right; we could have been thirty ahead if he had kept playing. It's incredible because I'm not under the illusion that I could have beaten Matlock head-to-head then. Matlock was one of the country's most feared bar table players, reaching a point where nobody wanted to play him on a bar table.

That's my account of one of the most powerful 1-2 punches I've ever been involved with. If I had Wade's break all the time, my game would have been lethal, but he was exceptional. I think he's still the only pro player to shoot a perfect match on Accu-Stats in the tournament finals and was the professional player of the year. I got to know Wade well, before his passing on one Christmas Eve outside Knoxville, Tennessee. While on his way to see his daughter, he was involved in a fatal car accident. I miss Wade; his wisdom will carry on through me forever.

Death Left and the Synchronistic Path (1986)

I remember it like yesterday: I was in a tournament in Hutchinson, Kansas, pushing myself to the limit and staying up for four days. Jeremiah Johnson became a friend of mine, and he ended up winning the tournament. I practiced with him before the event and was highly impressed with his skill level; he ran out like a beast.

This experience encouraged me to bet on him and win money before I finally blew it all, trying to give Little Joe the wild eight ball. I got 5th place in the tournament, but that last match with Joe cost me all my money; we played 18 straight hours after I'd been up over three days, and by the end, I was hallucinating, literally! I had enough cash to get down to Dallas, Texas, so I ended up driving down there to try to get pumped back up.

I was sitting in Rusty's Billiards on Northwest Highway, where all the big gamblers hung out. There was a chance to win a lot of cash there. Sitting at the bar with no money or gas in my car, I was too shy to ask people for money; it felt hopeless. I didn't have the nerve to beg; we call it "biting" in the pool world, so I sat there thinking, "What in the world am I going to do?" I was never religious, but in situations like this, the belief in a Higher Power was essential; I didn't know what "It" was, but I'd felt the presence and knew it was real.

Looking back, the one thing about life is how well everything connects. Things that seem bad from your perspective at the time can easily change your life into something even better; I've seen this act out over and over in my life. "Wow, if that didn't happen exactly like it did, it wouldn't have brought me all these good things or positive experiences." This is one of those cases.

As I sat there drowning in uncertainty about the future, guess who walked in the door? Jeremiah Johnson and his sidekick, Larry Landers. It looked like I'd seen an angel. I jumped off the barstool and ran up to Jeremiah, and after catching up, I told them, "I'm completely broke. I have no money and very little hope, but that's why I'm so glad to see you guys. Maybe we can join forces and win some scores together. I'm busted, but I'll assure you I can be trusted, and I'm hittin' 'em good!" This was the best sales pitch I could come up with in my state of mind. One thing is for sure: I was always a straight shooter in more ways than one!

"Oh, sure. If you get a game, we'll put the money up for you; let's team up and see if we can get you pumped up again. Do you have any spots close to here?" Jeremiah asked; I could see his mental wheels turning. I told them there was a spot in Paris, Texas, ripe for the picking, but I had someone who would play me right away, and I wanted to get at least enough money to eat and drink without borrowing from them.

They backed me against a local shark, and we played a set for $500, which I won. The deal we made was that the player would get 40%, and the other two would get 30% when any of us got action. I had $200, which seemed like a fortune to me then. Like many pool hustlers, the guy I was playing acted mad, threw a pool ball and put on a dramatic show. You've got to watch some seasoned pool hustlers; they will make a show to get a specific outcome. You've got to be on your guard, and that's really what this guy was doing because about 30 minutes later, he said, "Come on, I'll play you another set!"

But when I got up there to play, I was cold and not in the right mental state. Sure enough, he came back and beat me, and there I was, back to square one without a dime in my pocket. But at least I would have a roof over my head and wouldn't be starving anytime soon.

The next day, we decided to go to the spot in Paris, Texas, a little town Northeast of Dallas. We played the bar owner there, and I got him hooked and betting high. But the guy had no money; he's playing on the wire, meaning we're giving him credit. Since he owns the bar, we figure he's good for it.

I ended up beating him out of close to $6000, but of course, I didn't get any money, so he wrote us a check, and I'm still penniless. In times like this, it's best to keep a good attitude, but honestly, it is character-building; it seems like the most challenging situations in life end up being the most rewarding somewhere down the road. We got up early the next day and went into the bank with the check he gave us. Man, she cashed it like gold; I wanted to hug her! So now, suddenly, I had 40% of the $6000; after expenses, I still had $2200. I felt like I was rich.

Jeremiah Johnson wanted to fly back to Las Cruces, NM, where he stayed. Larry and I drove their car there, and I left my car at a friend's house in the back of his driveway. So, on the way, we played in several spots that I'd written down from other hustlers at Rusty's in Dallas. We ended up winning another $3800. So now I've got about $3700 or close to it, and we're in Las Cruces, NM. That's when my life changed because they set me up with a match against a guy there, the legendary Death Left. To my surprise, he was quite a character and owned a cemetery, so they called him Death Left. He was left-handed, of course. So thus, the name.

I played him the next day, starting a new chapter in my life because I met many lifelong friends in New Mexico. Death Left and I became great friends and made much money together. If all these things had not happened in the way they did, I don't think I would have gone to Las Cruces and met Death Left and all the great people I met in New Mexico. That started a fantastic new period in my life, worth much more than all the money someone could have given me at the time in Hutchinson or Dallas, where I was dead broke, and things seemed hopeless.

So, I think you'll see that in your own life. They say nothing's good or bad, depending on your perspective. The key to life, I think, is when these so-called bad things are happening, you do not let them affect your perspective and look at the good qualities that this experience may bring into your life because, from my experience, it always does. These days, I try to see it sooner.

Bizarre Killer Pilot Flies Plane with Flat Tires (1986)

I've been around many underworld characters, and one of the most memorable was in Albuquerque, New Mexico, where my mother lived for two years. I used to see many friends in Las Cruces and El Paso. But Albuquerque is where I met the most unusual one; he liked pool but was primarily a gambler and a golfer. I'm not mentioning his name—it won't be that hard to find if you do a little research, but for the most part, I will keep the names to myself to protect the innocent because let's just say that this does get a little hairy.

I started messing around with this guy in Albuquerque, a big golf gambler who played well; he'd beat some tour pros, like Fuzzy Zoeller, playing for money. He was a birdie machine; even lagging fifty and sixty-foot putts, he threatened the hole every time. Jerry was a supernatural talent until he started going off on the wrong path, and I will tell you this for sure: drugs will mess up your golf game. And your pool game, too.

But the last time I saw him play, it wasn't pretty. He hit it over one sand trap and back over the green into another. It was disappointing to see somebody get like that. It seemed like fun at the time to go over to his house; he always had hot girls in the pool or playing pool, but I could sense there was a dark element to this scenario, and drugs were undoubtedly the key factor.

I was infatuated with his success, especially the respect and fear that he elicited from people. According to him, he'd sold more real estate than anybody in the history of Albuquerque. He was also one of the first developers to promote and sell real estate on Padre Island in Texas by getting Paul Harvey, the famous radio personality, to promote "The Rest of the Story" on Padre Island.

Paul Harvey was paid to tell this story on his radio show and talked it up. At the time, this little-known island was a crappy place, but because Paul Harvey was trustworthy, they were able to change this public perception. He told his listeners Padre

Island was the best unknown secret in the country, "an unpolished jewel." Because of this marketing ploy, Jerry and his group sold significant real estate there for substantial money, apparently in the millions!

One night, we were at Jerry's house partying, and as usual, we stayed up all night. He was bored because none of the girls showed up.

"Let's fly up to northern New Mexico. I have a place up there by the Colorado border."

I was always spontaneous, but this proposition caught me by surprise. "You mean right now?"

"Yeah, I got my airplane at a private airport. I can take it anytime I want." Before I could stop, the words came out of my mouth, "Sure, that sounds like an adventure."

I asked him a few questions after agreeing, but I was under the influence and wasn't reasoning, so this sounded like a lot of fun and an excuse to keep partying.

We got in his BMW and raced to the airport. Jerry drove like a bat out of hell. It didn't feel dangerous; I just presumed he had too much money to die in a car crash. We pulled up, exited the car, and approached his plane. The first thing I noticed was that the plane wasn't sitting level; there was something off balance. Then I saw he had four semi-flat tires!

"Well, I guess we can't go. You don't have enough air in the tires."

Jerry didn't hesitate to say, "Oh, that'll be alright. We can still take off without air in the tires."

"Are you serious?" Even in my buzzed state, this didn't sound right.

"Yeah, yeah, yeah, it won't make any difference in an airplane."

Well, you know, I was drinking and feeling no pain then, so I went along with it, and sure enough, we took off without all the air in the tires. It was bumpy initially, but he had no trouble getting the plane up in the air. We're flying over impressive mountains up to Northern New Mexico to a spooky, creepy area. It's where they found cattle with all their insides taken out using laser-type precision.

There was a lot of paranormal and UFO activity in the area. My friend started discussing the national parks around here, which have 24-hour rangers that look for UFOs. At this point, I felt like I made a bad decision, and the more I got to know this guy, the more I understood why he liked this type of area. He was into some dark, satanic stuff, too. I was too young and naïve to understand that; it was like being in a movie.

We're about 20 minutes from where we're going to land, and that's when the bright idea came to me to ask, "What about landing without air in the tires?"

He looked at me, eyes noticeably dilated, and smiled, "You got a point there. That might not be so easy."

He calls ahead, and I'll never forget how uncomfortable it was to look down as we're landing, and there's a fire truck and ambulance with their lights on. That doesn't give you tremendous confidence when you're landing in a plane with no air in the tires, and they've got an ambulance waiting for you. Somehow, he landed that plane. It was a little rough, but he landed it; it felt like we were riding down a flight of stairs, and then, in the end, the plane jerked to the left, swerved around 180 in the other direction, and stopped.

Man, I got out of that plane as fast as I could. "Listen, I am not flying back to Albuquerque in that thing. I don't care how much air you put in the tires!"

"I understand. You know, that was a crazy thing, but we made it. I'll have someone drive a car up here tomorrow from Albuquerque."

He had a super cool house there. We picked up where we left off with the partying and spent the next day at the lake on his boat. That area was eerie. The mountains surrounding the lake were massive, and the scene looked like something out of a King Kong movie. They call New Mexico the Land of Enchantment for good reason.

I have many fond memories of that State, especially Donny Haney, whom we called Death Left, his wife Debby, all the friends I played golf with, at Picacho Hills Country Club and the Triple R Bar downtown, and of course, Larry Landers and Jeremiah Johnson, who introduced me to everyone at Tommy Izzo's house.

I was attracted to a young lady in Albuquerque named Charmin. She was a country western singer and a knockdown, gorgeous brunette. Jerry wanted her, too; however, she liked me romantically, and we started secretly spending nights together at her apartment. After that bizarre plane trip, I started feeling funny about being around Albuquerque, so I called Weldon Rogers and arranged a road trip with him.

My instincts were spot on; Charmin ended up being there when he took a bookmaker that I had met, handcuffed him, drove him up to the mountains with her there, and shot him in the head.

The next day, she flew to Mesa, Arizona, to get away, and the FBI somehow found out and immediately went and got her. He was on the run for a little while before they arrested him. Then my mother called me and said that she had just seen him on a TV show, the FBI's Most Wanted List top-ten, and that he had escaped jail.

The last time they heard from him, he was seen putting golf clubs in a black Porsche and speeding away. He had so much money that he got into a kind of country club-type prison, so escaping wasn't that difficult. His daughter or some girl snuck him a key in prison, which allowed him to escape.

He was on the run for several years, and they finally caught him in Hot Springs, Arkansas. This is where he went to hide, and he didn't look the same. I saw pictures of him when they caught him and returned him to jail. I'm pretty sure they will never allow him to get close to escaping again; he will undoubtedly die in prison.

I'm glad he never caught me with that girl. A friend of mine who knew the man said, "He would have taken you out in the desert and buried you up to the neck and put honey on you so that the ants would have eaten you slowly. I've had a lot of close calls in my life, and I think my Guardian Angels were working overtime in Albuquerque, New Mexico.

WORLD SERIES OF TAVERN POOL IN LAS VEGAS, NEVADA (1986)

I was 21 years old, living in Florida at the time, and scoring a lot of gambling matches. TR McIntosh was putting some money up for me as my Stake Horse. TR was a giant of a man and weighed in at one time over 500 lb. He had an incredible sense of humor, and because of his size, he didn't get out much, so he developed an amazing "gift of gab" on the telephone. I learned a lot about the ability to communicate and engage with people by listening to him.

He would call places, and they would ask his name, and he would say "Armondo Farfadidi" in a funny accent; he would make them repeat the name a couple of times, looking at me with a big shit-eating grin all over his face. He was always making me laugh and was genuinely a nice guy, but I wanted to be on his side when it came to gambling, and I think the feeling was mutual.

He pressed me to go to Vegas and play in the World Series of Tavern Pool. It was initially called Light Beer World Series of Tavern Pool, but they backed out, and Bud Lite took their position as title sponsor. As a result, the prize money dropped significantly, but TR still wanted me to play. The older players who steered me around to big-money games didn't want me to expose myself because they knew, as well as I did, that once I received national exposure, it would be difficult to get me into as many sweet cash games.

TR suggested that I use one of my fake names for the tournament, but I knew that wouldn't work because they would check my ID, especially if prize money were paid out. You must be twenty-one to enter this MGM Grand Casino tournament. Then I realized that no one knows my real name. I have been using CJ all my life, but my first name is Carson, and I am named after the famous Old West frontiersman and hunter Kit Carson.

I am supposed to be related to him and have always felt a connection. To me, pool hustling is the modern-day version of the gunslinging outlaw. While in Sante Fe, New Mexico, I traveled to the Santiago E Campos U.S. Court House to see his statue. It always makes me smile to think he must have been one straight shooter to get a statue erected in front of a federal courthouse.

I arrived in Las Vegas a little apprehensive and tired. My nervousness culminated into minor fear as I entered the MGM Grand Hotel. I had never played in front of a large audience and never felt I did well with large groups of people watching me. I always liked the seedy little pool hall at the end of an alley full of smoke and big gamblers.

This was not my present calling, so walking into the MGM Grand, full of lights and the sounds of slot machines and beautiful women serving cocktails, was way out of my element. I entered the tournament area and checked in as Carson Wiley. After filling out my entry form and paying the hundred-dollar entry fee, I turned a corner and entered an enormous room filled with one hundred brand-new Valley bar tables. With their sleek design and green felt, these seven-foot beauties graced one of the biggest arenas I'd ever seen! Ten rows of ten tables each, well-spaced for maximum efficiency and movement around the table. It gave me an intense feeling seeing all these pool tables and the stage was set; I would not have predicted what was about to happen.

The tournament consisted of ten rounds to reach the finals, with a single elimination race and two out of three sets per match. The final was best three out of five sets, race to four. I won every set until my ninth opponent, Pat White. Pat was a strong player out of Canada. He and I met in Detroit a few times, so I knew him and his game.

Fortunately, I came out strong and ran the first rack. I got snookered behind the eight-ball in the second set and had to kick out. He made a great bank and ran out to win the second set. We were now one-for-one going into the third set and a chance for the finals. He broke and didn't drop a ball, leaving me a chance to run out – which is precisely what I did.

I played Bill Eigel in the finals. Bill was a good semi-pro player from Los Angeles, just a notch below players like Earl Strickland or Buddy Hall. But today was my day, and I played flawlessly and beat him in a straight-set victory. I was so nervous before that final. I went to the bathroom five times like I'd drank a gallon of water! There were also over 500 people in the stands, which made a difference, but controlling my nerves was a skill I'd developed.

After the tournament, there was a media buzz about me because no one had ever heard of Carson. I was like this kid coming out of nowhere, winning first place in a major tournament. The media was having a field day, and one of the questions that kept coming up was about how aggressive I was on the table, rarely playing safe.

My response was, "The best defense is a great offense! I started playing 8-ball and 15-ball Rotation on a nine-foot Brunswick table at the age of seven. Playing 8-ball was second nature to me."

Another reporter asked me, "Where did all this confidence come from?"

"I just decided 100% of the time that I will run out every rack—there is no need to play it safe; you just gotta make those little balls in those big, big pockets."

After the big win, we started partying, and I ran into an old friend of mine, Scotty Townsend. Scotty was a road player from Louisiana who I'd run into all over the major gambling areas of the country. He was a tough, macho man, a colorful character who wrested alligators and had a Cajun flair. His friends in West Monroe said he could lift a car if you bet a fifth of Jack Daniels.

He always wore cowboy boots, just like me. We both didn't dress like typical pool players. He was a country boy; we got along well and had mutual respect as fellow warriors. If you were going to play Scotty, you had to be willing to win all the money he could lose or entice a Stake Horse to wager. Like he used to say, "I've never lost a pool match; I've just run out of money a few times!"

This was the truth. I tested him several times. We played long gambling sessions, sometimes over 20 hours, in Alabama, Mississippi, Tennessee, and Kansas. The last time I played him was in Florida, down in the Panhandle. I spotted him the wild 8-ball on a nine-foot table and won, but his best game was on the seven-foot bar-sized table.

We met in Vegas at the tournament, but not intentionally. We were both looking for gambling games but decided we wouldn't go against each other this time; we would partner up. The real action was being made after the tournament with gamblers from all over the U.S. The place was ripe for the picking, especially for seasoned road players like Scotty and me.

We started drinking in celebration and had a few drinks. When I say a few, that's a considerable understatement. Scotty could drink. We had champagne, mixed drinks, and beer. Afterward, we went down to the tournament area and were approached by some Mexican champions from California, strong bar table specialists. Not as strong as Keith McCready, Keith would gamble with them, giving them the seven or six ball, but they played well and kept woofing at me to play, but I was too hammered. However, Scotty said, "I got just the right buzz; what do these straight shooters wanna bet?"

"Really? Are you sure you can play right now?" I asked, trying to focus.

"Oh yeah, no problem." I peeled off $2000 to stake him and said, "Good luck, shoot 'em full of holes, Scotty!"

I wobbled over and sat on a pool table, laid back, and passed completely out. I don't know how much time passed, but I was suddenly shaken and disoriented.

"Wake-up! Wake-up!" I looked up, and it was Scotty's whisky breath in my face, "Come on, it's time for some more victory drinks."

I got up, not knowing where I was for a second, "What happened?"

He showed me this big wad of money and said, "I busted 'em, and the party is on!"

We went back to the bar, "Scotty, how in the fuck can you drink this much and play pool?"

"Oh, that's nothing," he said.

"One time, I drank so much that I pulled myself over before that long bridge down in the Atchafalaya Basin in my truck because I couldn't drive straight! The police came up to me, gave me a breathalyzer test, went back to their car for a while, and then they came back." I asked, "What did it read?"

The cop said, "Well, according to this, you're dead!"

Scotty was an incredible man, but he lost his life in a motorcycle accident. It's sad, but we had some great times together! I played in the Scotty Townsend Memorial Tournament and won third place over several champion-level players. I was happy about that because I felt like he was looking down at me, hoping that I would have a flashback and he could see that "Atomic 9-Ball speed" that we both had hit so many times when we were full-time road players.

THE REAL COLOR OF MONEY (1987)

In the mid-'80s, there was a lot of pool gambling in the country; my timing to be on the road was ideal because the movie The Color of Money came out; I'm sure many of you have seen that movie. It created a boom in the pocket billiard world. Upscale billiard clubs were opening, and many people who ordinarily wouldn't have gotten into pool started playing because they saw Tom Cruise spinning that stick and Paul Newman giving a lifetime performance. Critics would say it had some faults, but overall, it was a great movie, mainly because my friend Keith McCready co-starred as the legendary pool hustler Grady Seasons.

The Color of Money is the sequel to The Hustler, another great pool-themed movie in which Paul Newman plays Fast Eddie and Jackie Gleason plays Minnesota Fats. Experiencing this movie opened the door for many people to start playing. You could get critical and say that it created a bad reputation because of gambling, drinking, and drugs, but that was a realistic setting. However, the movie was amazingly well done!

It was good for the game to show the underworld elements because it was exciting, mysterious, and entertaining. New York Fats became Minnesota Fats after this movie, which was a genius move by Rudolph Walderone Jr, the real name of who played Willie Mosconi on Wide World of Sports, which originally inspired me to play pool at the age of seven.

When the movie came out, I was running the roads full time. My partner and I had worked our way through Kentucky and ended up in Pittsburgh, Pennsylvania. We had heard that the owner of this bar loved to play pool, back other players, and gambled for high stakes. At that time, I wore fake glasses and had an ID to conceal my identity.

We stopped at a store, got directions to the place, and pulled up in the parking lot. We mapped out a game plan; I put on my fake glasses, and we walked through the door into the establishment. We sat at the bar and ordered a couple of beers. The owner walked up and talked to the bartender, so we asked him if anybody there would gamble playing pool.

He looked at us suspiciously and said, "Can I see your IDs?"

"Do we need an ID to gamble playing pool?" my partner asked him, jokingly.

"No, I've had some law enforcement people come in here giving me a hard time about gambling and I just want to ensure you're not one of them."

We showed him our IDs, and he instantly lit up and said, "Yeah, I gamble playing pool. I love gambling, like in The Color of Money." He said, "You saw that movie, didn't you?"

I said, "Yeah, we saw the movie."

The bar owner continues, "I have a table upstairs like the one in the movie. Did you see the Gold Crown tables in the movie, they are the best!"

"Yeah, we saw the tables in the movie," this guy was totally obsessed with the movie; I could tell.

He took us to the end of the bar, where a small door opened to a narrow staircase leading up to a room above the bar. As he walked up, he turned and said, "Yeah, you'll love this table. This table is just like in The Color of Money. You saw the movie, and I'm pretty sure I asked you that."

We were like, "Yes! We saw the movie." I couldn't help smiling—this guy had no idea what he was getting into!

He was just stoked from watching that movie, and like I said, it greatly influenced people because it was exciting and showed the underworld of pool as well as it could. It created a lot of excitement and became the perfect storm for me because that's what I was doing, but I was the real deal. We reached the top of the stairs, turned a corner, and entered this small room. A Gold Crown Brunswick pool table stood in the center.

Glowing in excitement, he exclaims, "See, see, this is just like in The Color of Money. If you want to play some, I'll play you a race to seven for $100."

I said, "Sure, okay, I'll do that."

I kept the fake glasses on and played the set for $100. He didn't play very well; he couldn't run three balls in a row, so I beat him in two sets for $200. Then he called downstairs and had one of his bartenders come up and play, and I beat him.

Then he had another local guy come up, and I beat him. After that, he just started running all over. One of the best bar table players in Pittsburgh walked in, and a hush came over the room.

I knew him from a description, but he didn't know me, so I had a decisive advantage. I'd beat everybody up there on that 9-foot table. The owner approached my partner and said about the best player in Pittsburgh, "He'll play this kid some 9-Ball and bet as high as you want, but he wants to play on a smaller bar table downstairs; he's too old for these tight pockets."

What do you think? I could feel the anticipation; we'd been waiting for this. "Yeah, yeah, I'll do that." I felt that feeling that's getting me prepared to run out every time; I know what's fixin' to happen, and it's time to get the cash!

So, we went downstairs. I told my partner, "These glasses are bothering me. Can you get my contact lenses out of the car?"

We already had it rehearsed: I went to the bathroom, splashed water on my face, rubbed my eyes, and came out. I gave my partner the contact lens case and the glasses so people could see; it was all part of the show."

He took the empty contact lens case and the fake glasses to the car and removed the evidence. I didn't have the glasses on; they thought I'd put contacts in. This was a built-in excuse that my game could suddenly get better.

By this time, the place was packed, the word had gotten out, and everyone was there to bet on the hometown hero. My partner went around the room taking bets and writing them down in a notebook to keep track of the money; we ended up betting high; he was betting at least ten people on the side.

We ended up winning close to $7,000; much of it was from the owner, the one I talked to initially, who was so stoked about The Color of Money. He came up to me with a bewildered look and said, "You know, kid, you played a lot better at the end than you did at the beginning."

I looked him square in the eye and said, "Well, you saw the movie, didn't you?" His forehead turned beet red as he realized what had happened. I motioned to my partner, and we headed for the door. Sometimes, I count my blessings that we could pull these hustles off and leave with the money, but it had a lot to do with the element of surprise, how we carried ourselves, and good, old-fashioned luck.

STABBED (1988)

One night, a group of us were gambling in my pool room. We used to play pool, pitch coins for money, and play cards, and sometimes, there would be a dice-throwing proposition or two, but that night, we wanted to extend our gambling.

We all decided to go down to South Dallas to a gambling room that my friends knew about. I went with a guy named Black Larry, Reuben, and a small group we used to run with. South Dallas, also known as South Oak Cliff, is not a good area of town, but they knew the guys who ran the games and felt comfortable with his backroom establishment. I always felt comfortable around all ethnicities because Dallas has a high Hispanic and Black population, and I was raised without prejudice.

We went down to this gambling house on the second floor of this person's residence. Looking around as we walked up the outside stairs was typical inner-city decay. Old homes are sewn together with old, dilapidated fencing—large dogs barking in the distance. As we walked in, the place was packed with mostly Mexicans and Blacks, so I stood out as the only Anglo in the whole second-story house. My friend knew the owner, and he walked up and introduced me with the standard introduction and respect given for allowing us to play in his place. Everything was cool. I could sense the electricity in the air as a large black guy yelled at his dice!

The house was divided into rooms, and different games were played in each. The shag carpet had well-worn paths entering each room with the smell of Swisher cigars and stale beer throughout. A couple of rooms were dedicated to cards, and one was specific to dice, with a makeshift bar set up where the kitchen would typically be.

We grabbed vodka, jack, and beer from the bartender and confidently walked into the dice room. I put my money on the table and waited my turn to throw. About every five minutes or so, a cocktail waitress would come by. She seemed too young to work in a place like this but probably was related to the owner, so I tipped her well, and she returned promptly with a new drink.

We threw dice for a few hours, broke even, and had too many drinks. I swayed down the stairs and got in my blue 300 ZX to return home just as it started raining. The area had an eerie fog, like the kind you see in a B-horror movie that always foreshadows something sinister. I pulled quickly into a gas station on the neighborhood's edge to get some cigarettes, but the place was locked tight, with bars on the windows and large concrete blocks protecting the front door.

I knew I was in a very dangerous part of town, but my retreat mechanism has always been slow to engage. I paid the old man for my cigarettes through a small window and returned to the car. The fog had thickened, which made my vehicle hard to see only thirty feet away. In addition to the low visibility, my heavy buzz caused me to stumble as I approached the car door.

I heard footsteps approaching from behind within a foot of grabbing the car door handle. I turned only to feel the knife penetrate my left temple. As he sliced open a large wound, a flickering light from the canopy showed a pair of brass knuckles with an eight-inch blade attached to one end.

Blood immediately started gushing out of my head, and I instinctively covered it with my hands as the second strike went deep into my stomach, dissecting part of my spleen. The old, black man from the store burst through the door and screamed, "Get away from him, or I'll shoot!" The sound of a pump shotgun echoed through the parking lot, which I'm sure he kept under his register for protection.

The fight or flight instinct immediately kicked in, and I decided within a micro-second, "This is my chance to escape!" As I strained to focus, I reached for my door handle – pulled myself inside the car, and wiped the blood out of my eyes. The world was spinning, and the fog was so heavy that I could barely see the road. My left eye was useless as the blood streamed from the open cut above my temple, but I experienced no pain as the adrenaline coursed through my veins. I started the car and pressed the accelerator to the floor, jumping the curb and trying to control my car fishtailing as I frantically turned the wheel in the direction of my impending spin.

At this point, I had no conscious control of my body; my subconscious had taken over. The zone that had saved me in so many pool matches was kicking in again, but this time, it was no game; it was life or death! It seemed like I drove about five blocks with time stopped; I could feel my pulse pushing blood from the open wound in my head.

"I need to relax!" I told myself.

My heart was pumping rapidly as I pulled into another gas station, barely stopping before I hit the concrete barricade that secured the entry to this convenience store. With one hand over my bleeding temple and one hand over my stomach, I stumbled up to the window, which also had thick bars guarding the man inside.

"Help me!" That's all I could say.

The guy turned with a horrific look on his face. Sticking his head out of the small window, he looked both ways and motioned me to the side door. As I reached the door, it opened, and a small orange table was directly in front of me, where I presume employees could eat their lunch out of the view of customers.

I barely reached five feet with the man helping me to the table. I laid my head down and passed out. The paramedics awakened me as they moved me from the table to the stretcher. I was so tired I could barely keep my eyes open.

As the six men were putting me in the back of the ambulance, I had a moment of clarity; looking up at one of the men, I asked, "Am I going to die?"

The man looked at me directly into my eyes and said, "We don't think so."

My subconscious mind rapidly calibrated him for congruency. He seemed to be telling the truth because if I thought he wasn't, I would not sleep; I would fight to stay awake to see the last minutes of my life! I let myself drift off to sleep, only to be jolted back to consciousness by the men taking me out of the vehicle and racing me into the emergency room of the hospital.

Before I realized what was happening, I was on a table with a doctor stapling my bloody scalp back together, closing the sliced wound in my scalp, and then the stab wound in my stomach just a couple inches below and to the left of my naval. I felt little pain as my body had produced a large amount of a morphine-like chemical that stopped the discomfort.

The doctor came in after they got me stapled up; he looked at me and said, "You must have a guardian angel," as he put his index finger and thumb close together and looked at the small space between them.

"You came this close to dying twice tonight, and that, young man, is a miracle!"

The stab wound to my stomach nearly severed my spleen, and the laceration to my head came within millimeters of rupturing a major artery behind my ear.

That was one of the most brutal experiences I could have ever had. Still, many years later, I realized it was also one of the greatest because of two significant things: It changed how I felt about death and got me training in martial arts like my life depended on it.

I decided to go all out, whatever it took, and become an unstoppable pool-playing machine. This was the preparation I'd needed to face the next primary phase of my life, which led to me playing in the ESPN World Open, being selected as Player of the Year by Pool and Billiard Digest, and being named the Best Money Player of the 20th Century by Billiard Digest along with Earl Strickland and Efren Reyes.

To be continued...

Made in the USA
Columbia, SC
13 March 2025